**DATE DUE**

| | | | |
|---|---|---|---|
| | | | |
| | | | |
| | | | |
| | | | |
| | | | |
| | | | |
| | | | |
| | | | |
| | | | |
| | | | |
| | | | |
| | | | |
| | | | |
| | | | |
| | | | |
| | | | |
| | | | |
| | | | |
| GAYLORD | | | PRINTED IN U.S.A. |

# KEYWORDS | Nature

**OTHER**

Other Press • New York

Copyright © 2005 Alliance of Independent Publishers, France

First published in China by Shanghai Literature and Art Publishing House
First published in France by Éditions La Découverte
First published in India by Sage India
First published in Morocco and Lebanon by Arab Cultural Center of Casablanca/Beirut
First published in South Africa by Double Storey Books
First published in the United States by Other Press, New York

Production Editor: Robert D. Hack
Text design: Kaoru Tamura and Natalya Balnova

This book was set in Joanna MT by Alpha Graphics of Pittsfield, NH.

10 9 8 7 6 5 4 3 2 1

Library of Congress Cataloging-in-Publication Data

Keywords : nature / Chen Shao-Ming . . . [et al.].
        p. cm.
    Includes bibliographical references.
    ISBN 1-59051-109-3 (pbk. : alk. paper)   1. Nature   I. Chen, Shao-Ming.
        QH81.K45 2005
        508—dc22

2005007548

# CONTENTS

# SERIES PREFACE

Established on the initiative of the Charles Leopold Mayer
Foundation, the KEYWORDS collection was born of a propi-
tious encounter between a Chinese, an American, and a French
publisher. The project is now being executed by the Alliance of
Independent Publishers[1] that, besides its founders—Shanghai
Cultural Publishers and La Découverte in France—includes
Double Storey Books in South Africa, Le Centre Cultural Arabe
in Casablanca and Beirut, Other Press in the United States, and
Sage Publications India. The project offers fundamental notions
from different cultural points of view, taking a hard look at a
common object with a view from afar. The collection thereby
aims to produce an intercultural dialogue and an exploration
of globalization with, as point of departure, local points of

---

1. See www.fph.ch and www.alliance-editeurs.org

view on essential themes such as *experience*, *gender* (or masculine-feminine), *identity*, *nature*, and *truth*. Thus, in their respective languages, the publishers will provide the same small book on one of the words chosen beforehand, and each will then consist of six articles of about twenty pages each. For example, the notion of *truth* will, in turn, be tackled by an African, an American, an Arab, a Chinese, and an Indian writer, each of whose texts will then be translated into four languages respectively: English, Arabic, Chinese, and French. The texts will be exchanged between the publishers to come out under a same title within the same year in each of the countries in question. In short: one word and six points of view to create, if not a world, at least a book.

Such a new and difficult project had to proclaim its experimental character with all that this implies as source but also as experimentation and approximation. Furthermore, it needed a pragmatic framework and a few guiding, though equally flexible, principles. Then there was the choice of words. For some of these, we were concerned with current events, taking into account major political considerations, examinations divided along the line of contemporary debate in the terms and contexts of expression that are frequently misunderstood. The questions of *identity* and *gender* became imperative: these past few decades they have heavily mobilized public opinion and the academy. They are keywords that now circulate almost everywhere and deserve to be torn from the untrammeled use they so often get. They have gained from being set free from the ambiguities and globalizations that render them meaningless.

Obviously, the glitter of the topical is better understood when supported by a few historical and semantic reference points. By backing this up with symbolic patterns and antecedents, one can better define the outlines and what is at stake, check off implicit comparisons and their imaginary hierarchical

organizations, and get rid of old references that add up like hastily assembled arrangements. Thus, the false familiarities and
simultaneities, spun by the media networks, are seen more
clearly. In this plural space that has no center, in which the
suggestions may intersect or be ignored or excluded, the confrontation can only hold surprises. The map of problems, their
formulation, the development of ideas, the range of preoccu-
pations, the levels of historicity and abstraction, and the degree
of intensity necessarily fluctuate. Hybridizations are not always
recognized and identity fixations are not always where one
expects to find them. Gaps of temporality run through the
various societies themselves (and not just across borders) by
crystallizing other forms of discontinuity. The unspoken is at
least as significant as what is presented.

The complexity of the transmissions can never be sufficiently
assessed; therefore, the translations pose an immediate problem.
The concept of *gender*, which has nurtured entire departments
in the English-speaking universities and has henceforth been
adopted by international organizations, has always been the
object of controversy. It is of concern today in the United States
where it was born and spread, although not without polemics
in the feminist camp itself, because of the problematics of
transgender and queer. The Arab author will clasp it to do a
libertarian rereading of the past and brilliantly serve the cause
of women and homosexuals. As for the famous question of *identity*, which in its various modalities does not stop troubling politicians today, it has exciting extensions depending on whether
it is reopened to a very refined question on colonialism (Africa)
or refers to a game of mirrors and paradoxical deconstruction
that ends up as a transcultural demand (China); whether it lends
itself to a wholesome de-dramatization (on the side of the
Arabs) and a swinging back of the pendulum in the United
States as a reaction to earlier multiculturalism; or whether it is

simply the opportunity provided here to clearly expose the terms and turns of the debate (in India and Europe).

Other concepts, if not more classical and timeless, ask to be presented when they structure worlds, that is to say when they are articulated orders but also, for many people today, a haven on the horizon of a daily life in flux. Above all, when they turn out not to be any less problematic than the first ones: What is *nature* today? How did the Arab philosophers rethink the *physis* of Aristotle or the neo-Platonists and what advantage did the theologians take of this to fight them? How does *experience* issue forth from events in China and in what way is it inexpressable? Is it still pertinent to oppose scientific *experience*, the experience lived in psychoanalytic treatment, with what Kant calls the "judgment of experience"? Why has this term acquired such imaginary bulk in the portrayal that America has of itself? By what alternate routes have we moved from one model of mathematical *truth* and universal forms of what is *true* to a pluralization, indeed its disappearance as thematic in the order of the techno-sciences? How do we report in just a few pages on *truth* according to the Vedas, the Upanishads, the great epics, Shankara, the poetic theory of Bharata, the mystic songs of the *Bhakta*, and the Gandhian ideal? The history of ideas is not an insignificant exercise, especially in a limited space and for the benefit of the other who is presumed to be ignorant—or almost ignorant—of the background. Obviously, there will only be a few lines of demarcation here allowing for the decoding of a cultural landscape or of daily life, roughly outlining the genealogy of a philosophical question, and here and there letting the game of theoretic uncoupling or loans be guessed at.

It may happen that an author decides to ignore the historical side of a concept in order to focus on a reality that stands out: How and within what boundaries did the South African Truth and Reconciliation Commission operate? Generally, however, the issues have been put in perspective by being directed at an audience abroad and also by letting everyone hear the novelty of his or her own voice in hitherto unpublished combinations. In the absence or well nigh absence of a preliminary designation (methodological, epistemological, political, and so forth) the space that becomes visible is not without relief or accidents. Some articles may well seem too "technical," others not sufficiently so. From one region to another, they differ in their levels of analysis and more generally in their disciplinary approaches: the Chinese and the Arabs pay special attention to language; Indians like to think of themselves as sociologists or anthropologists; the plural disciplines of the American *cultural studies* differ from those of the French philosophers. These texts, which are neither encyclopedic articles nor free essays, have the value of being documents: they do not aspire to being strictly representative (of a state of knowledge, a discipline, an identity) and no institution mandated them, smoothed them out, or standardized them. Speaking for themselves, they call more than anything else for being discussed, studied, and augmented. It is left up to the readers to pursue the thinking, to immerse themselves in the different points of view to try to compare and flush out the dissimilarities or the common values. We are here concerned merely with providing some insights, with preparing an encounter, and opening a space to make contact.

The choice of authors was also the object of a few minimal guidelines. Priority was given to authors—philosophers, linguists, sociologists, anthropologists, and so on—from the South of the various cultural regions concerned rather than to those who live in the West. In this first series we did not always manage it, but for the most part this will be the case. Moreover, we have attempted to act in such a way as to avoid two stumbling blocks, each of which would misrepresent the project and both of which are well known since they feed the debate on globalization today. On the one hand, we had to avoid specific characteristics that were too great, whether it concerned terminology that was too specialized, subjective idiosyncrasies, or closed attitudes expressing a denial of the other. Although it is true that we do not all support certain political positions that are expressed here and there, on the whole we fulfilled this condition. On the other hand, we were not to give in to the standardization resulting from certain contemporary infatuations: identity withdrawal or mimetic reencoding in conformity with forms of a too-marked postmodern rhetoric. The collection rests on processes of scholarly circulation, the growing internationalization of research that solicited and stimulated it. It has updated a third more or less compact space corresponding to themes and regions that divert or complicate the dichotomies between dominators and dominated. Without this implicit theoretical horizon, the complex game of appropriations, occasional restrictions, and gaps that one sees emerge from one article to another, would not have been possible.

The achievement of these small books owes a great deal to the loyal support from and help of Etienne Galliand, to whom herewith our gratitude. We also wish to express our sincere thanks to Jean Copans, Françoise Cremel, Ghislaine Glasson Deschaumes, Thomas Keenan, Michèle Ignazzi, Michel Izard, Farouk Mardam-Bey, Ramona Naddaff, Jean-Luc Racine, and Roshi Rashed.

Nadia Tazi
Paris, November 2003

Translated by Marjolijn de Jager

from *Africa*


# AFRICA: HUMAN NATURE AS
# HISTORICAL PROCESS

———

Jean-Bernard  Ouédraogo

Translated  by
Robert  Bononno

> Listen more to things
> Than to beings.
> Hear the voice of fire,
> Hear the voice of water.
> Listen to the wind:
> The sobbing bush
> Is the breath of the ancestors.
> —Birago Diop

**FOR MANY OF OUR** contemporaries Africa is the continent that best lends itself to an examination of nature, given its place in the world as a land that is currently intact but threatened with destruction in the immediate future. The black continent is an unfriendly universe of age-old barbarism that stubbornly refuses the progress offered by a dominating Western civilization. There have been a number of criticisms of such ethnocentric prejudices, but they should not mask the fact that the historical context, often deliberately misrepresented, is the required starting point for anyone wishing to understand the complex relationships between mankind and the environment. The ecological project, too focused on the protection of nature, has arbitrarily established a distinction between humans and the natural elements. Instead, I wish to consider the question from a relational perspective inscribed within a continuous dynamic of meaning. Ecology, as a form of attention directed toward nature, is itself based on the evolution of our relationship with the physical world. The status of natural elements has developed in parallel with our humanity, *which nonetheless remains a form of authentic nature*. The problem raised by the misuse of the innate (defined, in contrast to acquired traits, as equivalent to the natural) requires that we rethink the factual and conceptual contours of the concept of nature, which, from this perspective, is an essence. Incapable of historical evolution, nature and culture are for some hopelessly irreconcilable. Nowhere else has the conflicting relation between these entities been as pronounced as it has in Africa. For here, the still-limited use of mechanisms for interacting with the physical world makes visible the clash between humans and their environment, and highlights the forgotten process whereby human alterity is constantly being constructed.

It is well known that point of view creates the object. But determination of this relationship is complicated by the fact that the totality imposed by the anthropological perspective tends to smooth over any disparities of approach and weakens the urge to express a truly African perspective. For although the outlook formed by European culture needs to be examined before we can proceed further, its object requires a minimum of critical coherence. Regardless of how precise the response given to this two-part investigation, it must confront a key question: In what way does the natural participate in modern Africa? In examining the natural, we must also examine the ways African societies have been inserted into the contemporary world. It is along these borders that the identity and status of these confrontational elements come most clearly into focus. These point of anchorage, and the subversions they provoke, reveal the profound figures of the present and encourage us to advance our inquiry toward a radical search for human identity as it is being constructed on this continent. In one sense Africa would then become a total world, revelatory of the social process and, by expressing a recollection of human experience, would incarnate the universal. In this essay I have three immediate goals. I wish to show first, how the human mind confronts external reality; second, how the universe of natural elements relates to the historical reality of the subjects who think it and act it; and third, I wish to frame the relation to nature as established in Africa within a global perspective of engagement and distance vis-à-vis the physical world. On this continent, as elsewhere, since nature does not exist in itself, only a nature that has become manifest through thought and action is conceivable. As a corollary we can accept that the multiplicity of local histories can variously reflect this common situation and that African conceptions of the world are strongly influenced by the violent eruption of allogenic civilizations that have turned out to be bellicose, as aggressive toward their fellow humans as toward other elements of nature.

## DISSIDENCE IN NATURE:
## THE INVENTION OF HUMANITIES

The unanimous celebration of the genetic and spiritual unity of the human race should not lead us to overlook the fact that humankind's long and frequently painful affirmation as something distinct from nature—and therefore from other components of the physical world—is a complex process of the hierarchization of humanity. Such ruptures establish the differentiation by which, even today, our relationship to natural species, including the stages of our own evolution, is based. Our identification as humans is the result of a twofold movement of historic singularity: the distinction of genus through the creation of a classificatory order of all the elements of the physical world, and the distinction of sameness through the establishment of a cultural scale, based on an active positivism, responsible for determining our distance to the savage world. Notwithstanding the African desire to affirm the nobility of being black, we must recognize that slavery and colonization have produced images that lead toward a reinvestigation of an African humanity that has been contested by others, one covered by layers of humiliation and based on the moral effects of an ecological crisis. The question of the African's relationship to nature implies that we first acknowledge the consequences of these forms of dissidence, of the hierarchization of humanities by establishing, beginning with African history, the status of natural elements, including that of humankind itself. The content of this symbolic understanding of the world is the principal condition for the practical treatment of "things."

The attitude to the outside world is consubstantial with the process of hominization of our common ancestors. Although it is extremely difficult, in spite of the important discoveries in paleontology, to resolve the enigma of humankind's origins and its primitive contact with the world, it must be acknowledged that, even in that distant past the "thing" was the point of interaction for a multiplicity of relations—utilitarian, aesthetic, and religious. In that "uncertain region of time and space," certain hominoids slowly liberated themselves from the animal realm by enriching "their anatomical and physiological makeup with cultural traits"[1] to achieve the "simian horizon" of contemporary humans. At such *decisive moments* the human trajectory is marked by the interweaving of competitive but complementary links, which contrast the biological order with the artificial invention of human culture. This process of human autonominization consists of a variety of repetitive points of contact (nourishment, habitation, sexuality, and spirituality) between humans and things, which structure their march toward civilization. With respect to Africa, an examination of the present situation requires that we determine the dominant force that for four centuries has attempted to transform, technically and symbolically, African conceptions of nature. This dominating force is the force of Western capitalist civilization in its phase of globalization. When did it encounter African visions of nature and what did this forced cultural association produce ecologically? This return to the past is justified by the fact that the Western order that has attempted to conquer and socially control the peoples of the known world has succeeded as the advance guard of a distant history. This history has for many years been interpreted from a narrowly economic perspective, although it contains, and is in large part based on, the realization of an attempt to define and process the elements of nature. This process consists of a succession of dissidences, divisions with elements that have been intentionally maintained within a closed natural order, bound to "inferior" stages of the human process, while at the same time the advance guard of civilization, as is generally known, has defined itself through the dynamics of a new singularity. This reorganization of systems of affiliation constantly defines the status of the elements of nature just as it redefines the classifi-

---

1. Serge Moscovici, *La société contre nature*, Paris: Seuil, 1994; translated as *Society against Nature: The Emergence of Human Societies*, Humanities Press, 1976.

catory hierarchy of human beings in terms of gender, race, and social position.

In *Cognitive Foundations of Natural History*, Scott Atran[2] explains how, against a background of struggle between folk taxonomies and scientific classification in Europe, the process that led from naturalism toward the development of a "natural system" of correspondence resulted in a "comparison of life forms" on a global scale. By conceptualizing genus and species within the natural order through their codification into families and classes, the search for the secrets of the living world through empirical (morphological) or intellectual (analytical) intuition succeeded in creating a mathematical grid that exceeded local contingencies. The result was the creation of a unique global order, where the "concept of an extended great chain of being (*scala naturae*) places mankind at one end of the standard and insects at the other as phenomenal residues."[3] Creation of this standard did not express a neatly defined enclosure of the identity of the human genus since, at the extreme end of this *scala santa*, the white race was established as the bearer of the most recent expressions of human civilization. According to this "masculine" way of thinking, ever since ancient Greece women have been excluded from the *summum bonum* and associated with matter and the carnal instincts. They are, according to Ephesian Matron (1659), "the paradise of the Senseless, the Plague of the wise man, and Nature's great error."[4] The mechanical revolution initiated a break with magical thought and imposed a new order of reason; now humans had to look for "the pre-

---

2. Scott Atran, *Cognitive Foundations of Natural History: Towards an Anthropology of Science*, Cambridge University Press, 1990.

3. Scott Atran, op. cit., p. 20.

4. Quoted by Brian Easlea in *Witch Hunting, Magic, and the New Philosophy: An Introduction to Debates of the Scientific Revolution, 1450–1750*, p. 289 (Harvester Studies in Philosophy), Humanities Press, 1980.

cise notion of things" and nature was seen in terms of systems of measurement and classification that could be used for new forms of social utility.

The ecological project for humankind's new grasp of things is also ideological and political, and has always been so. Based on my earlier discussion, two aspects of this claim must now be considered. The first is intimately connected with humans' internal differentiation, which classifies human beings according to biological and cultural criteria together. The second, a corollary of the first, being a kind of instrument of those principles of classification, defines concrete modes of acting upon natural elements. According to this Western system of taxonomy, the European, whose color is "normal" and who benefits from a perfected body and mind, is the bearer of moral superiority. By "ascending the color scale," affirmed Dr. Charles White, member of the Royal Society, "we arrive at the white European, who, being the furthest from brute creation, can thus be considered the most beautiful of the human race."[5] At the other end of the scale is the black person, the African, recognized as being the still unfinished product of human evolution, someone primitive, or "natural." According to commonly held opinion at the time, monkeys were found at the bottom of the ladder, possessing only rudimentary mental capacities; then came "the orangutan, the prototype of man and the Negroes of Guinea."

With the beginning of European expansion, when slavery and the conquest and colonization of Africans were in force, we find implicit or explicit taxonomies whose new frames of perception and interpretation of the world justified such treatment of newly conquered lands. Divided between a nostalgia for Mother Nature and a barely hidden desire for plunder, the conquerors of the imperial age invaded the most distant lands

---

5. Easlea, op. cit., p. 297.

in search of treasure or the souls of savages to domesticate. The *ordo mundi* of medieval Europe viewed the world as revolving around the Christian West, that "island universe," and distant Africa participated in this as a terra incognita populated, as the teratological fables would have it, with monsters of all kinds. It was the "poor world," the "land of shadows and realm of Satan." The discovery of America reinstituted earlier concerns about the unity of the human race, which seemed to have been resolved in biblical beliefs and theories that were defended in the natural history of the Ancients. According to representations current in those distant periods, the diversity of the world, which had been uniform since the earthly paradise, was derived from some form of corruption (Cain, Babel). This was reflected in the various cynocephali, anthropophages, and other monsters that always presaged some malefic fate. An important idea governed this critical period of European history: "Given that humanity as a whole descended from Adam, any physical deviation from the norm existing in Europe could only be explained by degeneracy, decadence, or as punishment for sin."

Similarly, the process of identifying a second human nature, as established by Enlightenment philosophers and naturalists, led to a renewed investigation of the unity of humans and, consequently, the diversity and hierarchy of the human race. The definition of the state of evolution of the society of humans resulting from a "second birth" contrasts the republic guided by reason with the state of nature, which in turn is contrasted with the primitive state, the realm of cruelty, the empire of the savage, the "stupid and limited animal." The criteria that define the advance of reason are exclusively local. People, like plants, according to current notions of intelligibility, are overcome by an implacable logic that continuously manufactures a range of exotic elements according to a hierarchy established in the West. So-called natural law, modeled on physical criteria, legitimated the conquest of non-European peoples, who were classified, according to the dominant racial stereotype, by their degree of resemblance to an ideal type, cultural and physical, that had been established by Western thought. Naturally, the shock of the primitive, by calling into question the degree of humanity accorded to every people encountered, imposed the idea of progress and thus the modality of admission into the great family of human civilization. But this theological debate became biological and cosmological, and then moved toward a geographic understanding of the world. Gradually, the fabulous geography inherited from the Ancients was replaced by the concrete geography enriched by the narratives of travelers. This conception of difference presented a problem to the West and pushed it toward proposing a solution that was both practical and symbolic.

It is important to recognize that this ideology, prior to framing the entire world, was first applied to European populations themselves. Helped by science, the rational society of modern Europe considered the mass of artisans and peasants as basic raw material from which a cultivated elite could withdraw wealth. To dominate the social underclass and other natural elements, the program to appropriate nature continues to make use of science and technology. Even today Pierre Bourdieu has observed the way in which the working classes have been relegated to the natural world as part of the process of politically legitimizing the ruling classes in Europe. He postulated the existence of a "relation that also entails the body and the soul, between those who are only nature and those who acknowledge their inability to dominate their own biological nature, their legitimate claim to dominate social nature."[6] The exploitation of nature occurs

6. Pierre Bourdieu, *Distinction, a Social Critique of the Judgment of Taste*, p. 573, Cambridge, MA: Harvard University Press, 1984.

according to the degree of humanity recognized in every form of life, animal or plant. Thus, a symbolic order is developed to legitimize the activity that would soon be undertaken through conquest and colonial domination. This period of global exploration corresponds, in the history of Europe, with the development of capitalism. The exploitation of forests, mines, and large-scale human labor intensified. The new system pushed Europe into a profound ecological crisis that was subsequently imposed on the entire world. Samir Amin[7] emphasized that, in this type of analysis, we must consider the ecological crisis as a consequence of capitalism but not yet as a crisis of capitalism itself. The capitalist ethos would engage these new opportunities the way pirates and brigands assaulted new territories to enrich themselves by any means at their disposal.

This history of conquest, although unique, does not yet reveal how the rhetoric of the ideology of domination expressed itself in Europeans' desire to establish the superiority of their race and civilization. Of course scholars and generals appropriated the framework of the dominant representation of the world, but this could be attributed to the logic of the capitalist period, which by and large denotes the power of process in action. The kinds of societies this system engendered have quite clearly defined the modalities of interaction that exist between humans and their environment.

The history of the medieval contradictions that led feudal Europe toward capitalism is well known.[8] While the limitations of feudal society led to crisis, the "solution" provided by capi-

---

7. Samir Amin, "Les conditions globales d'un développement durable," in *Quel développement durable pour le Sud*, Alternatives Sud, Vol. II, No. 4, Cetri/L'Harmattan, 1995.

8. See Jason W. Moore, "Nature and the Transition from Freudalism to Capitalism," *Review* 26(2):97–172, 2003.

talism brought with it the seeds of a new social crisis, with important ecological consequences. The exhaustion of the soil through the intensity of feudal production led to a decrease of revenue for the owners of farmlands. The solution was sought in the discovery of new lands, and this search was extended through colonial expansion. The search for farmland and agricultural products had to take into account the geographical conditions likely to interfere with the planned exploitation. Nature was the source of profit but was also an important obstacle to European expansion. Aside from the diseases that killed large numbers of sailors and soldiers in the colonial armies, in certain lands, the colonization of local populations was impossible. In more arid lands ecological enrichment was incompatible with the local situation. In all cases the force of nature has always been an objective limit. Baron Gourgaud, who traveled through Africa in the 1930s, wrote, "I would have liked to show many things. . . . But man's greatest enemies are the smallest: mosquitoes, tse-tse flies, ants, ticks."[9]

It was within this context that the colonial project began, leading to a profound transformation of African societies. One of the most important characteristics of the exploitation of new colonies consisted in plundering their natural resources. Raw materials, as they are now called, were extracted and transported to the coast for shipment and refinement in the West. This reality, which was long concealed because of political considerations, is essential for understanding the ecological crisis that accompanied imperial political domination. As with other elements of the natural world, dominated peoples suffered the same treatment and were integrated into a symbolic scale of development according to which the values of all the identified realities were

---

9. Quoted in Pierre Leprohon, *L'exotisme et le cinéma*, p. 60, J. Susse, 1945.

distributed. With this scale of values in mind, a system of legal and technological conduct consolidated all the things now made available through colonial conquest. In this sense colonial intervention is based on a rigid hierarchy of the elements of the physical world, and makes this new collection another available and exploitable resource. Conquest thus subjected humans, flora, and fauna to a system of intense exploitation. As a result, development, from the very beginning, brought with it an ecological crisis of major proportions.

## PROXIMITY AND COSMOLOGY IN AFRICA

To better understand the ecological effects of colonial expansion on African societies, we should examine the interaction between humans and nature on the continent prior to large-scale European intervention. Contrary to the assumptions of anthropology, which always sees the element of primitivism as foremost, we should perhaps insist on the fact that the status of natural elements is established by a social dynamic that is locally defined because it is connected with a global dynamic. In this context can the modification of the social value of nature be considered a function of an ancient ecological heritage and the ways it interacts with the newly introduced European system? By first examining the indigenous ecology, we can avoid introducing a falsified African viewpoint, based on exclusively European historical and symbolic frameworks.

Contrary to common belief, in Africa, as elsewhere, social space has never been monolithic. Social changes have delineated cultural and political orders that are different and sometimes opposed. From this secular fragmentation various ecological regimes have arisen, special relationships to nature, that correspond to prevailing political standards. A historical ecology of

African societies, therefore, must take into account the interaction of two complementary tendencies: (1) the primary mode of qualifying the elements of nature, including human beings; and (2) the political system and the techniques it uses to assure the reproduction of the social order. The study of community structures over a long period of time can help define a narrower common relationship in the African conception and use of natural elements. It is obvious that this cannot mean reproducing an ahistorical static vision of Africans' relationship to nature. Rather, we must try to grasp the internal dynamic as it took shape at the time of colonial activity to better understand the meaning of the ecological disturbances that resulted from outside intervention.

Paleontology shows that in the long process of hominization, the genus *Homo*, in becoming upright, spread the use of fire; eight thousand years ago, African society in Libya began to pasture its flocks. A millennium ago, in what is now Mauritania, humans left millet imprints on the pottery of the sedentary people they would soon become. Through the tools and technologies they acquired, these new people escaped biocenosis and developed the ecosystem by making it increasingly friendly. Recall that in those distant times, anthropogenic pressure was relatively low. Groups of human were sparsely scattered and migrated in search of resources in their immediate environment, having little major impact on it.

We can state with some certainty that the level of technological development of precolonial African societies resulted in a relatively balanced relationship between humans and their environment. The modest level of technological advancement and the still generally low level of demographic pressure helped them avoid destroying the potential of the natural world, so common today. Their relationship to nature was largely based on a particular conception of the world order and people's role in it. By considering the historical conditions of the evolution of people's relation to their environment, we can illuminate the reciprocal influence between ecological factors and the consequences of civilization. Although it is difficult to establish with certainty the makeup of the plant population in Africa, we know that it was initially related to the forms of contact and intermingling of indigenous populations. Although part of the existing plant cover was dependent on the lengthy evolution of the planetary ecosystem, a number of plants were transported and transformed by the mobility of human populations. The history of the peopling of Africa not only illustrates the most important human classifications, but also traces the dynamic of the relation of humankind to nature and of the evolution of selection, of the composition and maintenance of the immediate plant environment. Natural elements intervened in various ways in the lives of people, although it did not appear useful, theoretically or practically, to define an impermeable boundary between these two orders of reality. Ultimately, an examination of this history leads to the conclusion that our analysis should emphasize humankind's "circular" integration in an ensemble composed of things and beings.

Although this aspect is too often exaggerated, the African vision of humans' relationship to the physical world reflects a kind of statutory, historical interdefinition of people and things. The variety of African social situations expresses a diversity of relations between humankind and the elements of nature. Here I will examine a handful of significant examples. According to a number of African symbolic systems, the relationship between humans and the natural environment engages the entirety of social relations, including the connection to dead ancestors and the spirits who people the forests and sacred woods. The local universe is experienced as a continuous process that is conceived and organized as an integral whole. The precolonial African world integrates the use of plant and animal resources as part of a general relationship to the world. Moreover, not only is the world peopled by physical things, but also in nature the spirits rustle and murmur and express themselves in harmony with the world of the living. Embedded in the lengthy course of the natural order to which humans are subject, we consider the activities of production as simple variants of a process associated with Mother Nature. Therefore, it would never occur to humans to contradict nature without taking an infinite number of precautions—the consequences of inappropriate meddling are serious for the individual at fault as well as for the community.

For the Pygmies the forest is the realm of spirits; here the terrifying souls of the dead become immaterial forces. Humans must abandon these places, which have become the abode of invisible powers and are reserved for spirits who have returned from the beyond to animate the forest realm. There they monitor the proper conduct of humans. They are also their ambassadors to the inhabitants of the forest. The Aka pygmies consider the manes to be the real masters of the forest and its resources, under the direct control of the supreme Being. They supply humans with their subsistence by driving the animals toward the hunters. In some cases the spirits appear during periods of crisis, to calm dissension and preserve the cohesion of the group. Thus humans' itinerary cohabits fraternally with that of other living things. Lengthy observation of these ecological processes leads to the creation of a taxonomy and the identification of practices that must ensure the general equilibrium of the world. In this context no boundary generally exists between the behavior of humans and the rhythms of nature. Medicine and agriculture, for example, are methods for treating problems, sometimes pathological, affecting plants, animals, and humans. It is common for the reproductive health of plants to be associated with that of humans.

In reality the interdependence between ecological processes and human life cycles, which are integrated in this world, is established on a daily basis, and we are familiar with the causal connections postulated between human sexuality and plant reproduction. In some communities a menstruating woman who accidentally comes into contact with crops considered to be in an "advanced stage of pregnancy" can lead to sterilization of the woman or the loss of the harvest. According to the same logic, sexual relations are often forbidden in the bush because the unchecked intermingling of cycles of reproduction will disturb ecological harmony. Similarly, there is a direct connection between human behavior and the animal and plant world. Adultery on the part of a hunter's wife can directly influence the availability of game, which the bush will refuse to provide because of the transgression.

This type of representational system sees no major difference between nature and society. The continuity of this world, as presented here, is not free of rules of identity and correspondence. Ecological harmony is normative. In central Africa the master of political rituals has ecological power over the equilibrium of temperature, and the temperateness and humidity of the lands under his political control. Similarly, warfare incorporates a strategy of destabilizing the adversary's ecological system. The religious order is also connected to the ecological order. The cult of the ancestor culminates in establishing good relations with the dead, whose discontent leads to unpleasant consequences not only socially but ecologically. The interface between the visible world of humans and the invisible world of ancestors and gods is provided by nonhuman intermediaries, the djinn, who have often chosen to dwell in trees, woods, hills, and ponds, and are sometimes incarnated in animals. The religious function inscribed in nature protects it against the abuse of humankind. Brush fires, overcutting, and fishing are often under the protection of the ancestors, who may prohibit practices that degrade the environment. The interaction of plant processes with human activities means that control of the natural world is a source of power for people. Among the Diola of Senegal, for example, the hunter is also a doctor, and the guardians of the sacred woods have real power over society. For the Ntomba fishermen of Zaire, the water spirits talk to the fisherman in dreams, as he sleeps, to remind him that any overfishing will be counterbalanced by the gift of a human life. The exploitation of natural resources requires the agreement of religious institutions, which regulate humankind's relationship with the physical world. Many African societies have a pantheistic concept of nature, which is conceived and experienced as a living being, inhabited by supernatural beings and living creatures, with whom human societies must get along.

In this universe, where individuals are highly integrated into the social fabric, strict discipline and social control provide cohesion and ensure the social and physical reproduction of the group. To the ordinary way of thinking, no sense of property, and therefore no individualistic appropriation, is tolerated. The community considers itself the "beneficiary" of available resources. Access to them is authorized within the limits established by the community of people, placed under the authority of the spirits. In such a system a powerful feeling of communion with nature serves as the foundation for the durability of the group. This animist world, integrated in the ecological process, is vulnerable as long as the meaning on which social activity is based has not yet made a radical break with magical thinking. Humans experience the violence of a world they think they share. This world, which is not the idealized one of the "good savage," subjects people to the precariousness of the unforeseen and often leads, depending on the uncertainties of ecology, to murderous confrontations. A lack of intelligence, profoundly marked by a fear of the natural order considered as a threat or an offer, is not a universally accepted model for integrating the elements of the natural world. A number of simplistic considerations obstruct the face-to-face confrontation between humans and the third dimension. This world is subverted when the encounter with the exterior, with Western logic, provokes a moral crisis and the subsequent withdrawal of traditional values, and an economic crisis caused by the commodification of social relationships. Exposure to the world of capitalism has led to an increase in technological potential, which augments the capacity to extract natural elements for the benefit of an increasingly rapacious market.

## COLONIAL DEVELOPMENT:
## "GREEN IMPERIALISM"

Concerning the French colonial effort, Jean Loup Amselle[10] has shown the function of "republican raciology" in French colonial expansion in Africa. Paradoxically, this colonial policy devalues the native and overqualifies natural elements. The white man who penetrates Africa maintains considerable distance, both physical and cultural, from the African, who remains a filthy savage. Specialist anthropologists of colonial Africa maintain and disseminate a vision of a continent inhabited by beings moved by spontaneity, the instinct that keeps them bound to the animal kingdom. Marcel Griaule, discussing a film made about the Dogon, wrote, "The shots were all taken in real time as if it were an actual newsreel. The locals must not be asked to reconstruct or even rehearse anything. For them, everything is spontaneous,

---

10. Jean Loup Amselle, *Vers un multiculturalisme français. L'empire de la coutume*, Paris: Flammarion, 1996.

and if we embarrass them with details, they are lost. . . . The Dogon are excellent actors. They all have an instinct for the public arena and each has his own way of reacting and manifesting the feelings he experiences."[11] From first to second nature, Africans' animality is present to express the consistency of their behavior as something innate. During the early stages of the colonial conquest of Africa, one of the most committed officers, A. Baratier, expressed, in his florid and unambiguous language, the representations that established France's civilizing mission. He saw the black woman as the "savory fruit of the Sudan" and referred to the indigenous population in these words: "These natives are equally still, their waist elongated by a long boubou of Guinea blue, they watch the steamboat (progress) drift by; and these beings without needs, without desires, probably wonder what has led us to the Sudan, failing to understand our activity as much as their inactivity."[12] The natives, who have no needs, no desires, no activities, are not humans. Since they do not belong to the great family of humans, they cannot know love: "How could the Blacks love? They have no words to describe it. They are unfamiliar with the most gentle of verbs, cannot conjugate it or can do so only as animals do." Thus confused with untamed nature, the African becomes an element of nature, ripe for development in those conquered territories.

The negation of the African's humanity lies at the origin of this differential treatment, which is based, as indicated above, on a historical foundation tied to the evolution of European societies. Industry has been imposed in Europe and America as the principal engine of modern society, and industrial

---

11. Quoted in Leprohon, op cit., p. 185.
12. Quoted by Jean-Bernard Ouédraogo, "Scénographie d'une conquête: enquête sur la vision plastique d'un colonial," *Les cahiers du LERSCO*, special issue, September 1991.

products have played a central role in those societies. The price of noncommodity products, those not yet "transformed" by people's skill, are continually declining. Africans, who are not very productive, have become a burden for the colonizer. Without being able to radically deny their presence, or exterminate them, the colonizer has used them to produce and transport natural resources. Today, Africans, who are no longer a precious commodity, are weighed down by their "savage" customs, against which Western religion and education have been mobilized.

The great administrator of the French colonies, Robert Delavignette,[13] studied the consequences of the colonial policy that consists in inventing a new kind of African, who, during the next stage of colonial exploitation, will become both producer and consumer. During this period of colonial exploitation, it was not so much a question of enlightening the indigenous peoples but of supplying them with the basic means essential to their new social vocation. So, for example, on the eve of independence, the Belgian colony of the Congo had only nine students. At the moment of colonial development, we witness an inversion of the values of "natural" things. "Nonhuman"[14] elements acquired great importance because of their usefulness for industry and trade. European demand grew and encouraged business to bring back from Africa the rare and profitable products the continent supplied in abundance. In this way, deep ecology was fostered in Europe, which focused on preserving nature and encouraged

---

13. Robert Delavignette, *Service africain*, Paris: Gallimard, 1946.

14. Even today we can appreciate the force of this objective preference in the nearly religious encouragement to export goods, which clashes with the rejection of immigration, seen as a scourge, and the strict control of the temporary free circulation of individuals.

the colonial system.[15] This has developed into a fascination with African botany and primitive life, the development of tourism, and, as a result, the establishment of policies for preserving a primitive existence that is often derided by the native population. In this sense we can understand how colonial activity might be viewed as a policy of appropriating natural resources such as reserves, forests, mines, and land. In some cases large companies and colonists have benefited from this confiscation of natural resources. To ensure proper resource management, during the 1930s a number of research centers and learned societies were created. The unresolved contradictions inherent in this system are still visible today in Kenya and more clearly still in Zimbabwe, which is trying, with difficulty, to control the problems created by a colonial policy of land appropriation initiated by white colonists. In a number of cases land colonization has transformed the local ecology by imposing the relocation and consolidation of villages and by encouraging the arrival of European hunters, all of which has helped to reduce the domain of the primitive and has led to a break in the ancestral equilibrium established between humans and the nature they cautiously exploited. Colonial hunting, or leisure hunting, which does not correspond to any existential need, has led to the extermination of species such as the jaguar and the blue antelope. The population of many animal species has diminished considerably as a result of colonial rapacity. In some regions pesticides have destroyed bee colonies. A situation such as this, in which the most precious commodity is no longer humans, leads to a tendency to discipline people as aids to production, in order to make use of them for the extraction and refinement of natural resources.

---

15. See William Beinart, "African History and Environmental History," *African Affairs* 99:269–302, 2000.

A number of traditional chiefs, representing the ecological universe of old Africa, have opposed such predatory policies. But as some analysts have noted, colonization has also led to the diffusion of vectors for new diseases. In turn, the success of colonial medicine has led to the elimination of infected areas in the savannas of West Africa, freeing up arable land and leading to intensive exploitation.

The focused policy of natural resource exploitation in the colonies has been indispensable to the European economy, which has greater need of raw materials than of labor. This has been verified since the decline of the economy of the slave trade, which focused on the development of productive crops, accompanied by an effort to acclimatize plants from other regions. The desire to economically reconvert these territories led to the development of experimental botanical gardens and protected reserves, organized from the very beginning of the establishment of colonial policy. In forestry, colonization applied a policy inspired by a European model that was based on the exclusion of rural populations. The colonial state, while facilitating the appropriation of natural resources, was preoccupied by their renewal in order to be able to secure resources and ensure their continued exploitation. We often forget that colonial policy was a kind of "green imperialism" (Richard Grove) in that its principal goal was the exploitation of the natural resources of the conquered territories.

As a direct method of extracting natural resources as well as people, this mode of exploitation intensified the development of what have been called "complementary economies" to satisfy the demands of the new economic situation. In reality, colonial development has primarily been a form of ecological predation. The dominant power is primarily interested in the utility of the goods offered by nature that are immediately available. In this way an international division of labor has been established: raw materials produced in Africa are transferred to Europe to be transformed and refined. In Africa itself the unequal availability of resources has systematically led to increasing regional division. The abundance and ease of access to export crops has helped guide policies for developing the colonial territory. The current development of the continent has been strongly marked by this "colonial ecology," which has handicapped efforts to implement current economic policies. In this way the coastal areas and regions that produce agricultural export products have benefited from greater distribution of agricultural policies, infrastructures, and market organization. The administrative and commercial structures inherited from this period perfectly express the system of ecological plunder. Forced displacements of populations were provoked to respond to the new organization of the colonial territory. The moderate use of nature imposed by the indigenous ecology was rapidly transformed through the logic of colonial accumulation. The essential element of this change has been the integration of natural resources into the pathways of commodity markets, which have since become part of the global market. People subjected by the dominant power have been forced to orient their activities toward the search for hard currency so desired by colonial tax services. Initially constrained by nature, then by money, they would become one of the principal factors of the destructuring of the old order. While the principal goal of colonial power has been to ensure the exploitation of local resources, indigenous peoples—there to do the master's bidding—have been used to construct roads, string telephone lines, maintain trails, and haul goods. This direct consumption of human life has subsequently taken an indirect turn. People were first a means before becoming subjects and then citizens of the postcolonial state.

This evolution corresponded to the establishment of a system of capitalist exploitation, which made people producers and consumers for the new market. Africans began their forced march toward agricultural production. Colonial policy demanded that every village produce, often in a collectively farmed field, cash crops that provided little to the growers. The purchase price was insignificant. The requirement that peasants grow cash crops profoundly modified the order of social values and introduced them to an unknown form of commodified social relations. Money became an essential element of all social transactions. These combined colonial pressures resulted in the imposition of cash crops that gradually eclipsed the growth of food crops. Through the abandonment of food crops for cotton and peanuts, a significant social imbalance was created. Fields and labor once dedicated to subsistence agriculture were now used for more profitable crops. When the Karaboro say that "cotton kills," they refer to the fact that the mass adoption of cash crops has significantly reduced subsistence farming and created hunger among the peasants. The imposition of profitable monocultures has decreased and sterilized the once commonplace living contacts with nature. Through this peasant proletarianization, the new social system has gradually but decisively incorporated them into the now globalized space of capitalism. The major ecological crisis experienced in the Sahel during the 1970s was one of the consequences of this ecological restructuring imposed by colonial development. The search for cash forced many peasants to emigrate to the coasts, where the colonists had developed a plantation economy and were exploiting forest lands. The new forms of production used on these large tracts destroyed countless plant species through the use of pesticides and massive deforestation. The ecological crisis that followed the application of this predatory policy led Africa, in the words of Joseph Ki-Zerbo, toward a "slow-motion apocalypse"[16] that has

16. Joseph Ki-Zerbo, *Compagnons du soleil*, Paris: La découverte/Unesco/FPH, 1992.

destroyed local religions, eradicated African languages, and eliminated the endogenous pharmacopoeia, through what has been called sorcery. Africa, which possessed the richest biotopes in the world, has undergone a form of genetic decay, while the West has developed gene banks from the precious wild varieties frequently collected on the continent of Africa. This ecological upheaval has not only led to the destruction of trees and the reduction of ground cover, it has brought about the eradication of entire swaths of African plant growth,[17] once intimately tied to the ecological cycles. Colonization, in the name of Christian values, has organized autos-da-fé of art objects and mystical African religions, leaving many populations without any spiritual defense.[18] The ecological harmony typical of thinly populated societies that are not part of a market economy has been broken once and for all. Obviously, during this confrontation, the indigenous ecosystem has lost the battle to the powerful destructive forces of colonial capitalism.

## THE MARKET AS AN ECOLOGICAL FACTOR

With the new social organization, the result of the confrontation of ancient societies with colonialism, a form of African modernity arose throughout Africa that was profoundly marked by the commodification of social relations. The old forms of community organization were torn apart, destroyed by a

---

17. Ki-Zerbo describes how the disappearance of certain plants that are hard to find because of drought but essential to the composition of ritual foods has led hunters to abandon many secular rites.

18. The example of the mass conversion to Catholicism of the Daagara of Burkina Faso is representative. See M. Paternot, Lumières sur la Volta (Histoire d'une peuplade africaine: les Dagari), Lyon: Plus Grande France, 1949.

powerful process of dividing individuals and incorporating them in new configurations, larger and more powerful, defined in accordance with the needs of capital. Now, commodity exchange informed all dimensions of social life and structured a new ecological order. The current ecological crisis brings into sharp relief the absolute priority given to the struggle for survival. Whereas in the past the ties between the human realm and the world of nature were based on immediacy and close proximity, commodity logic enforces distance and imposes the use of money as an essential condition for accessing the elements of nature. This ecological alienation forms the basis of the new social order and has determined the shape of the modern African social system. In the countryside the search for money has inevitably introduced into the system of values a new hierarchy of natural elements. The selected market, the new ecological protagonist, validates and invalidates every entity identified in the physical world. Whereas the indigenous ecology of self-subsistence inscribed mankind within a harmonious relationship with the natural order, the market society destroys this collective and nonmonetary proximity by reifying the environment, which is now a collection of merchandise offered for sale. Unfortunately, following the logic of the same system, there is no equal distribution of the capacity for access to resources, to the means of survival. The problem is that, like all commodities, the presence and, therefore, the availability of each natural element is a function of its value as a commodity.

The construction of highways has destroyed the local environment, and long columns loaded with wood for delivery to the cities offer the sorry spectacle of the coming ecological catastrophe. In the face of this calamity, caused by the new modernity, the destructive behaviors associated with traditional cultures—tree cutting and brush fires—appear as necessary means for regulating nature's exuberance. Through the use of pesticides and bulldozers, the African forest has been delivered to the world market for precious goods. Similarly, subsistence crops are sent to the urban centers of the West. Along with this come the inevitable natural disasters, which result in desertification and the loss of water in ponds and streams. Although sedentary societies have been most affected by the ecological transformation, nomadic peoples have also experienced crises of their own. André Bourgeot has analyzed the lengthy movement of pastoral peoples toward the break between ecology and economy. He notes that the imbalance stems from, among other factors, the separation of nomadic shepherds from the open range due to the development of commercial crop growth. According to Bourgeot, the long-lasting drought of the 1970s created a great divide—the impossibility of reproducing the conditions for "appropriating the use values of ecological nature"[19] and the definitive loss of the ability of pastoral ecosystems to organize, the basis of the renewal of those societies. Some studies have shown that through such external influence, the natural elements that were once valued in the local cuisine and, more generally, by local society, have now been abandoned and replaced by new cultivars in response to market pressure.

Technical skills have been made obsolete through the mass import of competitive goods. This is what happened in the weaving industry, which formerly used local cotton but is now threatened with extinction because of the easy availability of imported clothing from the West. In contrast, the disappearance of practices associated with shea butter was soon compensated for by the need for shea butter for the West's cosmetic industries. Consistent with this historical perspective, the relation between habitat

---

19. André Bourgeot, "Une rupture du couple écologie-économie. La crise du pastoralisme Touareg," in Blanc-Pamard and Boutrais, *A la croisée des parcours. Pasteurs, éleveurs, cultivateurs: Dynamiques des systèmes agraires*, p. 67, ORSTOM, 1994.

and environment is also undergoing transformation. The houses, huts, and tents suited to the local climate have been replaced by modern houses constructed with inappropriate materials. Now a new phenomenon can be observed in the transformation of habitat in Africa. Faced with the impoverishment of the plant environment and influenced by the large houses of bourgeois life, a growing number of Africans have been bringing plants into their homes. Ornamental and decorative plants are increasingly commonplace in living rooms and courtyards. An ecological culture is also emerging slowly, a substitute for the rarity of plant cover in the cities. It's possible that this domestic "reforestation" is the expression of a nostalgic return to a lost ecological past. The Western model imposes a specific form of dwelling, consistent with the dominant forms of domestic unity. The extended African family is replaced by a domestic model that is closer to the nuclear family dominant in the West. One of the consequences of this domestic transformation is associated with personal relationships. Affectivity emerges and shifts in order to correspond to the elective sentiment of the couple, distinct from the community, and to structure new political and associative relationships. In this way African sexuality, which was formerly governed by the community and associated with the search for friendly alliances, and social means of production and reproduction, has freed itself of community social pressure only to accept that of money. Humanity's relation to itself as the first ecological dimension has been subjected to the laws of the marketplace and has led countless young women into prostitution, seen as the last means of providing oneself with some form of social capability.

Although modern medicine provides for the efficient treatment of certain diseases, a new social fragility has appeared in the form of the acquired immune deficiency syndrome (AIDS) and its consequences, affecting both the system of production and reproduction. In reality, beneath the economic and social crisis that the continent is experiencing, an ecological catastrophe is slowly developing. The predatory economy has been put into practice by states or relatively organized groups of individuals, who are attempting to pillage the natural resources of entire regions. The deadly isolation of eastern Kivu in the Democratic Republic of Congo is one of the many examples of the misfortunes caused by competition for access to natural resources. The hasty evocation of the resurgence of ethnic identity in interpreting conflicts in Africa does not bear analysis. It is the competition[20] engendered by the commodification of society that is the heart of the problem. Ethnic identity is only one of the formal investments used. By becoming part of a commodity ecology, the indigenous ecology based on respect and preservation of nature has given way to extreme practices. These threaten people and the environment they depend on for survival. Modern Africans, no longer tied to a community and falsely inscribed in a fragile whole that has been hastily identified as the state, do not find the cohesion and ethical principles of the world they once knew. The new singularity sees no reason to maintain this ancestral and balanced relationship of humans with their milieu. What matters now is their disenchanted relationship to a physical world that has been transformed into a repository of goods. Entire regions have been disfigured (both in terms of human life and devastated nature) by the rush for gold, diamonds, and minerals of all kinds, which attract peasants and adventurers looking for easy profits. In fact, this forced entry into Western ways of life introduces cultural values that are easy to adopt but that require a financial capacity the local populations do not always have. On the one hand, the market appears as the

---

20. See Jean-Bernard Ouédraogo, *Violence et communautés en Afrique noire. La région Comoé entre règles de concurrence et logique de destruction*, Paris: L'Harmattan, 1997.

high-pressure urgings of a group, a way of life based on com-modity consumption, which has the force of law for the indi-vidual. At the same time, clear individual limitations are imposed on the ability to access vital resources.

In the towns, people's relationship to the elements of nature has been accentuated even further through the distance and mediation imposed by the market. Access to material and sym-bolic elements essential for social life is conditioned by the movement of money. Spaces cut into parcels have become the privileged object of intense transactions. The market now orga-nizes the individual and collective use of urban space. Waste management in African cities, which have become increasingly spread out, has become a central focus of urban ecology in Africa. The lack of established methods for collectively manag-ing refuse in cities (growing constantly) has had a negative ef-fect on air quality and prevents many inhabitants from leading a healthy life. In these various ways the life cycle of humans tends to become disconnected from the slow ecological process that formerly regulated human activities. In this older process, the methods of municipal management extend the policy of popu-lation exclusion, experimented with during the period of colo-nial development. The management of public assets benefits a small group of individuals who reproduce wealth-based hierar-chies, according to the extent of their financial capacity in a market society. The position of human beings, the central ele-ment of nature, is defined by power, an external thing. It is the economy that now structures the system of food consumption and determines the conditions of human reproduction. Take food, for example. The composition of foodstuffs has undergone a rapid transformation as a result of the import of products from Europe and America. Less expensive, they have replaced local products. The surplus fowl from the European Community that has invaded African towns and cities has replaced the regular consumption of game. Machinery has followed the same path. Second-hand cars that have been sold because of high levels of pollution in Europe make their way to Africa. The economy of taste as it is currently formed has introduced new food products, some of which are not even produced in Africa. They have condemned to extinction other plants and animals, whose consumption is made impossible by the recent but powerful culture of market exchange. An important consequence of adopting foreign culinary habits is the drastic and determined restriction of the range of African tastes, which are thereby diminished. The most recent generations are not even aware of the existence of many of the recipes, leaves, fruits, and animals now considered exotic but once used in the villages.

## CONCLUSION: THE INVENTION OF A HUMAN NATURE

There is no single concept of nature. In Africa several concepts coexist; indigenous ecologies come into conflict with the logic of predation invented by capitalist Europe. But each of these concepts incorporates a vision of the world and modalities for humans to act upon themselves and, consequently, on each of their components. Two main historical currents of human civilization struggle to govern the life of people. The point of view defended here supports the view that the African perception of the environment is intimately associated with the status of historical confrontations in defining values that govern beliefs and practices on the continent. The application of policies and systems of action in this context, whether positive or negative, always faithfully reflects this provisional equilibrium among social values. The sociologist Norbert Elias has rightly observed that "the evolution of the image that man creates from what we call 'nature' is one of the aspects of the overall evolution of human society."[21] His theory, which sheds light on my argument both practically and symbolically, claims that the concept of nature is the product of a long historical process of distancing that reflects the dynamic of societies. The slave trade, colonization, and the forced entry of the global market society have radically transformed the perceptions Africans have of their natural environment as well as the different uses it is put to. Gradually, Africans have moved away from the close, egalitarian relationship they once had with the elements of nature, to objectivize and externalize them; they now see them as increasingly distant from themselves, separated from the point of anchorage of their new humanity. This objectivization is also a way of commodifying the elements of nature whose value is established through a historical process marked by the triumph of commercialized social exchanges. Is it possible, given these overbearing constraints, to impose a different orientation on the way we process nature's elements? More than simply the subject of immediate political concern, nature is the foundation and product of our civilization, for it profoundly influences overall human behavior. It is urgent, therefore, that we attempt to humanize modern Africans by reconciling them with nature, and reconstituting their philosophical and technical identity, together with a concern for the other, both plant and human. This human nature we have sought for so long must now confront the indictment of the historical process that has led us to this impasse. How could it be any different when the order of things, rather than exalting the humanist spirit, forces us to suppress our instincts? The current disorder caused by humankind's influence on the environment reflects the dysfunction of African societies; it is only when Africans begin to learn the rhythm of nature that they will rediscover the

---

21. Norbert Elias, *The Court Society*, p. 259, New York: Pantheon Books, 1983.

harmony of a well-understood progress. Nature is the material and cultural foundation of social existence. Faced with the dangers that threaten Africa's future, it is time to rediscover an African sense of equilibrium, the careful use of the products of our environment as a required transition toward a renewed focus on the human. What is required is a utopian transcendence of the criticism of our current behavior, together with the rediscovery of universal brotherhood through the intervention of a new human nature freed of the foreclosure and egotism of the past. That is the challenge faced by modern Africa, now condemned to pursue a shared future through respect and solidarity with our total humanity—nature.

# THE IDEA OF NATURE IN AMERICA

———

Leo Marx

> *Yet Nature is made better by no mean*
> *But Nature makes that mean.*
> —*Shakespeare*, The Winter's Tale

**THE IDEA OF NATURE** is—or rather, was—a defining American idea. For some three centuries, in fact, from the colonial era to the closing of the Western frontier, the encounter of European settlers with what they perceived as wilderness—unaltered nature—was the dominant theme of American history, art, and literature. By the end of that era, however, wild nature was coming to seem a thing of the past, and images of the pristine landscape, a preeminent icon of American nature, nurtured a burgeoning nostalgia. Concerned lovers of wilderness, led by John Muir and Theodore Roosevelt, organized a movement dedicated to its conservation, and Congress set aside vast woodlands and sites of scenic beauty (Yosemite, Niagara Falls, Yellowstone) as national forests and national parks. By 1920 half the people lived

in cities, and as the green world became a less immediate presence in their lives, the idea of America's special bond with nature lost much of its credibility. Then, in the 1970s, with the
onset of the ecological crisis and the rise of the environmental
movement, a large part of the niche in public discourse occupied by the word *nature* was taken over by a relatively new,
matter-of-fact surrogate: *the environment*. During the 1980s the loss
of currency and status suffered by the idea of nature caught the
attention of a number of scholars and public intellectuals, and
by 1999 European specialists in American studies chose, as the
topic of their turn-of-the-century conference, "'Nature's Nation'
Reconsidered: American Concepts of Nature from Wonder to
Ecological Crisis."[1]

The topic is as daunting as it is timely. For one thing, the very
word *nature* is a notorious semantic and metaphysical trap. As
used in ordinary discourse nowadays, it is inherently ambiguous. It often is unclear whether references to nature are meant
to include or exclude people. Besides, the idea of nature has always carried the sense of essence: of the ultimate, irreducible
character or quality of something, as for example, "the nature
of femininity" or, for that matter, "the nature of nature." When
this second meaning is in play, it tacitly imputes an idealist
or essentialist—hence ahistorical—character to the particular
subject at hand, whether it be femaleness or nature itself. The
multiple meanings of the word testify to its age: its roots go back
(by way of Latin and Old French) to the concept of origination—
of being born. As Raymond Williams famously noted, *nature*

---

1. The conference of the European Association for American Studies was held
in Graz, Austria, April 14–17, 2000; the present essay derives from the paper
I gave there: "The Pandering Landscape: On the Illusory Separateness of Na-
ture in America." See Hans Bak and Walter W. Hobling, eds., *"Nature's Nation"
Revisited: American Concepts of Nature from Wonder to Ecological Crisis*, Amsterdam: VU
University Press, 2003.

probably is the most complex word in the English language.[2] Moreover, when the idea of nature is yoked with the ideologically freighted concept of American nationhood, as in the intellectual historian Perry Miller's sly use of the epithet *nature's nation*, the ambiguity is compounded by chauvinism.[3]

Contemplating the nature of nature in America has led many scholars, of whom the historian Frederick Jackson Turner, author of the influential frontier theory of American history is the exemplar, to adopt the contested idiom of "American exceptionalism." And not without good reason. However wary of chauvinism a historian may be, it would be foolish to deny that when Europeans first encountered American nature, it truly was, and to some extent still is, exceptional—perhaps not unique but, like Australia, a continent even less developed at the time of contact—surely exceptional. It was exceptional in its immensity, its spectacular beauty, its variety of habitats, its promise of wealth, its accessibility to settlers from overseas, and it was exceptional, above all, in the scarcity of its indigenous population. Hence the remarkable extent of its underdevelopment—its wildness—as depicted in myriad descriptions of the initial landfall of European explorers on the American coast. In those stock images the newly discovered terrain appears to be untouched by civilization, a strange cultural void populated by godless savages or, in short, raw nature.

From the beginning, then, nature in America was primarily regarded as an aspect of geography or topography. Nature was

---

2. Raymond Williams, *Keywords*, p. 219, New York: Oxford University Press, 1983.

3. Miller first used the phrase in his 1953 essay, "Nature and the National Ego," in *Errand into the Wilderness*, p. 209, Cambridge, MA: Harvard University Press, 1956, 1967. Later Elizabeth W. Miller and Kenneth Murdock used it as the title of a posthumous collection of Miller's essays, *Nature's Nation*, Cambridge, MA: Harvard University Press, 1967.

a terrain, a landscape, a place. Thus the meaning and value that arriving Europeans attached to American nature was determined by an amalgam of its physical attributes and their imported preconceptions. Every belief system they brought to the New World, every ideology that served as a rationale for one or another colonial system of power, embodied a conception of nature and of humans' relations with it. In what follows, I begin with three early American belief systems and the conceptions of nature incorporated in each. Each had its origin in Europe, and each represents a chapter in the history of the idea of nature in America.

But a preliminary caveat. I plan to focus almost exclusively on the role played by ideas—as distinct from direct sensory experience—of nature in American thought. This means, unfortunately, that I bypass the rich store of interpretation and representation of the natural world embodied in American literature and art. This somewhat arbitrary distinction is justified, first, by limitations of space and, more importantly, by the fact that writers and artists are chiefly inspired not by ideas of nature but rather by their own perceptions, sensations, and impressions of the beauty, power, and complexity of biophysical nature—the thing itself.

Puritanism: A revealing starting point is the Puritan leader William Bradford's well-known depiction of the Cape Cod shoreline as seen from the deck of the Mayflower on its arrival in 1620. He describes it as "a hidious and desolate wildernes, full of wild beasts and willd men."[4] Here the bias inherent in the Christian (and, in particular, Calvinist) idea of nature as fallen—as Satan's

---

4. William Bradford, "History of Plimoth Plantation," in Perry Miller and Thomas Johnson, eds., *The Puritans*, pp. 100–101, New York: American Book Company, 1938.

domain—effectively erases the humanity of the indigenous Americans. Bradford associates them with wild beasts.

The concept of satanic nature provided a useful foil for the sacred mission of the Puritan colonists. In 1645, for example, John Winthrop, lieutenant governor of the Massachusetts Bay Colony, used it as an ideological weapon to defend his theocratic authority. His enemies had charged him with infringing on their liberty, and in his uncompromising response in the General Court he develops the distinction between two kinds of liberty: natural and civil. Natural liberty, "common to man with beasts and other creatures," is the liberty, he argues, we enjoy in a state of nature, namely, to do evil as well as good; civil liberty, on the other hand, is moral, hence available only to the truly regenerate, only to Christians redeemed from sin by the reception of divine grace. According to Calvinist doctrine, only those rescued from the state of nature may enjoy the God-given liberty to do what is good, just, and honest. Here, on the coast of a vast, unexplored continent, the idea of an ostensibly separate realm of nature was a valuable rhetorical asset for the colony's leaders. Allusions to wild nature served to reinforce the doctrinal barrier between themselves, the elect, and the unregenerate whom they consigned to the realm of natural lawlessness. In the lexicon of Protestant Christianity in America, the essential character of primal nature was conveyed by epithets like "howling desert" and "hideous wilderness," and by the malign names— savage, cannibal, slave—assigned to indigenous peoples. In Winthrop's argument, accordingly, the unarguable existence of a separate (unredeemed) state of nature helps to justify his a priori condemnation of the unregenerate, who constitute a potential threat of lawlessness, anarchy, and misrule. Their geographical location underscored the theological argument: the only escape from natural unregeneracy open to them was the reception of divine grace.

*The Enlightenment*: By the time Thomas Jefferson wrote his draft
of the Declaration of Independence, the theological notion of a
dual nature, part profane, part sacred, was being supplanted by
the unitary nature of Newtonian science and deism. Here the
initial identification of American nature with the landscape is
expanded to embrace the natural processes, or laws, operating
behind its visible surface. Because the newly discovered celestial machinery obeys physical laws accessible to human reason,
Newtonian physics has the effect of bringing humanity and
nature closer together. Besides, the mathematical clarity and
precision of the new physics makes the old images of a dark,
disorderly nature repugnant. Alexander Pope summed up the
change in the prevailing worldview in the couplet engraved on
Newton's tomb in Westminster Abbey:

Nature and nature's laws lay hid in night.
God said, "Let Newton be!" and all was light.

By 1776 it made sense for a rhetorician as gifted as Jefferson
to extend the hypothetical reach of nature's laws—or, to be more
precise, of principles analogous to them—to the unruly sphere
of politics. To justify the colonists' acts of treason and armed
rebellion, he has merely to describe them as the means—indeed,
the only possible means—of claiming the independent status to
which they are entitled by "the Laws of Nature and of Nature's
God." Nature, as this free-thinking president conceives of it, is
not so much the work of God as God is a constituent feature of
nature. By invoking a secularized idea of nature on behalf of a
quintessentially political cause, Jefferson helped to narrow the
gulf separating humanity and nature.

But for that purpose, the idiom of the natural sublime was
even more effective. Nine years later, in *Notes on Virginia*, Jefferson
invoked the sublime to account for the unsurpassed beauty of

one of American nature's most cherished creations—Virginia's Natural Bridge. An ardent practitioner of the neoclassical aesthetic, Jefferson credits the beauty of the bridge to its symmetrical form or, as it were, to the strikingly close approximation of its form to ostensibly natural principles of order and proportion. He begins his description of the bridge with a detailed analysis of its exact dimensions, as if reported by a detached observer writing in the third person. But then, partway through, he abruptly puts himself into the scene, climbs the parapet, and, shifting to the second person, he describes how "you" inescapably would react if you too found yourself standing on the narrow ledge looking "over into the abyss."

> You involuntarily fall on your hands and feet, creep to the parapet and peep over it. . . . If the view from the top be painful and intolerable, that from below is delightful in an equal extreme. It is impossible for the emotions arising from the sublime to be felt beyond what they are here; so beautiful an arch, so elevated, so light, and springing as it were up to heaven! The rapture of the spectator is really indescribable![5]

As this passionate Wordsworthian apostrophe suggests—it was written about fifteen years before the preface to the *Lyrical Ballads*—Jefferson already was prepared to enlist in the Romantic movement. But even after the triumph of Romanticism, the separateness of nature remained a largely unchallenged if unstated premise of public discourse. Since no authoritative biological counterpart to the Newtonian laws of nature had yet been formulated, supernatural explanations of the origin of life were not yet vulnerable to the challenge of scientific materialism. By

5. Thomas Jefferson, *Notes on the State of Virginia*, p. 55, William Peden, ed., Chapel Hill, NC: University of North Carolina Press, 1955.

the same token, pantheism retained its status as a Christian heresy, and dutiful communicants were advised to be wary of the feeling of oneness with nature.

*Romanticism:* In 1836, four years after resigning his pastorate in the Second (Unitarian) Church of Boston, Ralph Waldo Emerson anonymously published *Nature*, which came to be known as the manifesto of Transcendentalism, a New England variant of European Romanticism. It was Emerson's first and only attempt to formulate a systematic theory of nature, and in it he probably came as close as he ever would to repudiating the orthodox theological assumption that humanity and nature belong to separate realms of being. To illustrate the effect of being in "the presence of nature," Emerson describes an epiphany that is patently irreconcilable with that assumption. One gloomy afternoon, while crossing the town common, he was suddenly—unaccountably—overwhelmed by a sense of immanence or, as he puts it, of "being part or parcel of God." It was a largely secularized variant of the Protestant conversion experience, and it suggests the possibility, as Emerson puts it, of an "occult relation"—or state of oneness—with nonhuman nature. The balance of *Nature* may be read as an effort to devise a reasoned explanation, or justification, for this transformative experience.

The epiphany expresses Emerson's passionate commitment to the idea of nature as a primary locus of meaning and value and yet, at the same time, his growing skepticism, on both theological and scientific grounds, about the received idea of a separate nature. As a Unitarian, to be sure, he already had repudiated most supernatural aspects of Christian doctrine, including the divinity of Jesus. A few years before writing *Nature*, indeed, he had resigned his pastorate on the grounds that he no longer could in good conscience perform the—to him excessively literal—sacrament of the Lord's Supper. At that time, moreover, he was studiously keeping abreast of the latest advances in geology and zoology

that provided empirical evidence for the emerging theory of evolution. When *Nature* was reissued in 1849, in fact, he appended a
new verse epigraph depicting humanity's origin:

> A subtle chain of countless rings
> The next unto the farthest brings;
> The eye reads omens where it goes,
> And speaks all languages the rose;
> And, striving to be man, the worm
> Mounts through all the spires of form.[6]

Emerson, like many of his contemporaries, was receptive to the
concept of evolution long before he read Darwin's *Origin of Species*,
but he was not prepared to abandon the idea of nature's fundamental separateness. That orthodox idea is built into the conceptual structure of *Nature*. In defining his key terms, the graduate of
Harvard Divinity School is careful not to sever the remaining ties
between his conception of nature and its theological origins.
Thus he postulates a universe made up of all that exists except for
one thing: the human soul. All being, he asserts, "is composed of
Nature and the Soul," and he goes on to specify that "all that is
*separate* [emphasis added] from us, all which Philosophy distinguishes as the NOT ME, both nature and art, all other men and
my own body, must be ranked under this name, NATURE."
Though he looked with favor on the general idea of biological
evolution, he remained faithful to the pre-Darwinian idea of nature as a discrete entity independent of humanity.

But of course it was the theory of humanity's evolutionary origin, as definitively set forth by Darwin in 1859, that made that

---

6. Ralph Waldo Emerson, *Complete Works*, Vol. I, p. 8, Boston: Houghton Mifflin,
1884.

traditional idea untenable.[7] On that score the logical import of Darwin's argument is clear and conclusive. If *Homo sapiens* evolved through a process of natural selection, if our species is inextricably embedded in a global web of life forms, then there can be no such thing on Earth as a separately existing domain of nature. But the logic of science is one thing, and ancient habits of mind are another. Despite the passage of some 145 years since Darwin first caught the world's attention, and despite the confirmation his theory has received, first and last, from an international consensus of scientists, the crucial fact of humanity's genetic ties with all other known forms of life has yet to be incorporated in prevailing assumptions about the nature of nature. In today's public and private discourse, including that of knowledgeable people who pay lip service to the concept of evolution, the idea of nature is routinely invoked as if it constituted a discrete, independent entity. As the historian of science Lynn White, Jr. noted in his influential 1967 essay, "The Historical Roots of Our Ecological Crisis," "Despite Darwin, we are not in our hearts, part of the natural process."[8]

But that is putting it mildly. The publication of the *Origin of Species* immediately aroused intense public hostility, especially among churchmen and religious believers. There was no way, finally, to disguise the truth: Darwin's theory flatly contradicted the biblical account of the creation. Besides, people of all persuasions, many nonbelievers among them, were—still are—revolted by the notion that we are kin to the higher primates. It

---

7. In *Origin of Species*, though Darwin's theory of evolution by natural selection remained incomplete until the publication of the *Descent of Man* in 1871.

8. Lynn White, Jr. "The Historical Roots of Our Ecological Crisis," in Paul Shepherd, ed., *The Subversive Science; Essays Toward an Ecology of Man*, p. 369, Boston: Houghton Mifflin, 1969. See also, Leo Marx, "American Institutions and Ecological Ideals," *Science* 170:945–952, November 27, 1970.

makes them feel, as they say, tainted by bestiality. So does the idea that humanity reached the pinnacle of the food chain by winning a long, murderous struggle—in the poet Tennyson's phrase, "red in tooth and claw."[9] But it should be said that the repugnance aroused by evolutionary theory did not surprise its wisest proponents. Years before he published the *Origin*, Darwin had acknowledged his fear that it would raise the specter of atheism. He clearly understood—and empathized with—the widespread impulse to deny, or gloss over, the disturbing implications of his theory. But he urged readers to resist the impulse. "Nothing is easier," he warned,

> than to admit in words the truth of the universal struggle for life, or more difficult – at least I have found it so – than constantly to bear this conclusion in mind. Yet unless it be thoroughly engrained in the mind, the whole economy of nature . . . will be dimly seen or quite misunder-stood."[10]

In America today the "culture war" that was mounted against the doctrine of evolution in 1859 seems to be waged as vigorously as ever. An organized movement of some forty-five million evangelical Christian fundamentalists tirelessly proposes local and state legislation to ban the teaching of evolutionary science, and to replace it with Creationism, a religious theory of human origins. The fundamentalists also constitute an influential faction within the political party, led by the president of the United States, that now controls the Congress.

But the perceived antireligious import of evolutionary theory was not the only reason for its failure to be accepted by the

---

9. "In Memoriam," (1850), which he had begun writing in 1833.
10. Charles Darwin, *Origin of Species*, p. 74, New York: Mentor, 1958.

American public. Even more important, perhaps, was the largely unremarked conflict between the Darwinian conception of humanity's embeddedness in natural processes and the nation's chief geopolitical project: the settlement and economic development of the continental land mass. As Alexis de Tocqueville observed, most European settlers were "insensible" to the beauty and wonder of the wilderness. "Their eyes," he wrote, "are fixed on another sight: [their] . . . own march across these wilds, draining swamps, turning the course of rivers, peopling solitudes, and subduing nature."[11] That westward march, aimed at transforming the continent's natural resources into marketable wealth as rapidly as possible, was executed under the aegis of slogans like "manifest destiny," "the conquest of nature" and, above all, "progress."

The belief in progress, a shorthand term for a grand narrative of history, probably was post–Civil War America's most popular secular creed. It held that our history was, or was rapidly becoming, a record of the steady, cumulative, continuous expansion of knowledge of—and power over—nature, a power destined to effect a general improvement in the conditions of life. On this view, nature's role in the unfolding of material progress is critical but entirely subservient to human purposes. It is an indispensable source of knowledge and raw materials, hence most usefully conceived as wholly other—an unequivocally independent, separate entity. The combined authority of the progressive ethos and the Christian churches probably explains most of the antagonism toward Darwinian theory and, by the same token, the popularity of the doctrine known as Social Darwinism. Though seemingly an offshoot of evolutionary biology, Social Darwinism was in fact a perversion of the new

---

11. Alexis de Tocqueville, *Democracy in America*, Vol. 2, p. 74, Phillips Bradley, ed., New York: Alfred A. Knopf, 1946.

science. It turned on the idea of the survival of the fittest, a catchphrase given currency by Darwin's self-appointed interpreter, Herbert Spencer. It was Spencer's popularized version of Darwin's theory that did most to make Social Darwinism a widely accepted rationale for free-market capitalism and, more specifically, for the ruthless practices of the robber-baron generation of American businessmen.[12]

The massive incursion of white settlers into the western wilderness dramatized their nation-building progress. In the collective consciousness the successive stages of that great migration were represented by an imaginary boundary—a moving boundary—that separated the built environment to the East from the expanse of undeveloped, ostensibly unowned or, as it then was called, "free" land to the West. Never mind that the land already was inhabited; the westward movement of the boundary represented the serial imposition of a beneficent civilization on unruly nature, including, of course, its "savage" inhabitants. The boundary was a gauge of progress, and in tacit recognition of its ideological significance, it was given a proper name—the frontier—and accorded iconic status as an actual line—usually a broken or dotted line—imprinted on maps and documented by demographic data regularly collected, revised, and published in official reports of the United States Census. Eventually the word and the icon were compressed into a single term, the frontier line, visual marker of America's conquest of nature. Conquest was an apt term for the process. After comparing America's treatment of nature with that of other nations over the ages, one historian

---

12. Richard Hofstadter, Social Darwinism in American Thought, 1800–1915, Philadelphia: University of Pennsylvania Press, 1944. See also Leo Marx, "The Domination of Nature and the Redefinition of Progress," in Leo Marx, Bruce Mazlish, eds., Progress: Fact or Illusion?, pp. 201–218, Ann Arbor: University of Michigan Press, 1996.

asserts that "the story of . . . [the United States] as regards the use of forests, grasslands, wildlife and water sources is the most violent and most destructive in the long history of civilization."[13]

It is not surprising that a people busily ravaging that western cornucopia had little use for the theory of evolution. The Darwinian view of human life as inextricably enmeshed in natural processes was not easy to reconcile with that destructive enterprise. What made the conventional idea of a separate nature preferable, under the circumstances, was its hospitality to virtually any set of meanings and values. Though most nineteenth-century Americans evidently thought of the national terrain as a hostile wilderness, tolerable only so far as it could be subjected to human domination, an eloquent minority favored an opposing view. A cohort of artistically gifted nature lovers, adherents of European romanticism, was prominently represented by Thomas Cole, Frederic Church, and the other painters of the Hudson River School; by Emerson, Thoreau, and a host of poets, essayists, novelists, and philosophers; and by conservation activists like John Muir, Gifford Pinchot, and Theodore Roosevelt. In the press and the popular arts of the era, morever, a sentimental cult of nature helped to vent the pathos aroused by the spectacle of ravaged forests, slaughtered bison, and vanishing Americans.

The ambiguity inherent in the idea of nature was a critical factor in determining the apocalypic outcome of *Moby-Dick*, Herman Melville's epic account of America's violent assault on the natural world. He was so impressed by the irrational, violent character of that assault that he instructs his narrator, Ishmael, to seek out its origin and its consequences. The inquiry rests on two implicit assumptions: first, that the relations between American society and

---

13. Fairfield Osborn, *Our Plundered Planet*, p.175, Boston: Little, Brown, 1948.

nonhuman nature are typified by whaling, a technologically sophisticated, for-profit industry devoted to killing whales; and,
second, that the psychic roots of the enterprise are exemplified
by Captain Ahab's obsession with wreaking revenge on one particular sperm whale whose distinguishing feature is his uncanny
whiteness. (The sperm whale, not coincidentally, is the largest
living embodiment of nature on the face of the earth.) But what
is it about the whiteness of this whale, Ishmael asks, that provokes
Ahab's ungovernable hatred? Melville devotes an entire chapter
to the inquiry—a chapter without which, Ishmael insists, the
whole story would be pointless.

After an exhaustive analysis of every meaning and association
of whiteness he can think of, it occurs to Ishmael that the uncanny
effect of the color—or is it the absence of color?—is not attributable to any one of its meanings, but rather to its hospitality, like
that of material nature itself, to myriad, often antithetical, meanings or, in a word, to its ambiguity. At times, he observes, whiteness evokes terror, disease, death, and at others "the sweet tinges
of sunset skies and woods, and the gilded velvets of butterflies,
and the butterfly cheeks of young girls." But then Ishmael recalls
that the beauty of natural objects is no more inherent in their
physical properties than their color is; actually, he realizes, their
seeming beauty is the product of the "subtle deceits" of light and
color, and that in fact "all deified nature paints like a harlot, whose
allurements cover nothing but the charnel-house within." All of
which leads him to conclude that Ahab's obsession is in large
measure attributable to the maddening blankness—the essential
illusoriness—of nature, its capacity to provoke yet endlessly fend
off his rage for meaning. In the end, the mad captain's anger
overwhelms his reason, and the tragic outcome, as Ishmael describes it, is an impassioned warning against futile efforts to grasp
the ultimate meaning of nature.

By the final decades of the twentieth century, the loss of status and currency suffered by the idea of nature was becoming obvious. Avant-garde artists and intellectuals took for granted its imminent demise. In an influential 1984 essay, Fredric Jameson, a prominent theorist of postmodernism, argues that the disappearance of nature was a necessary precondition for the emergence of the postmodern mentality. "Postmodernism is what you have," he asserts, "when the modernization process is complete and nature is gone for good."[14] With characteristic postmodern tendentiousness, Jameson assumes that nature is a cultural construction—a product of discourse—and emphatically not an actual topographical entity. From his idealist philosophical perspective, the dominant American idea of nature—nature primarily conceived as geographical actuality—is meaningless. In Jameson's view, that usage, with its tacit claim to being an exact representation of the biophysical world, is epistemologically naive. That meaning of nature is gone for good, he is saying, precisely because it epitomizes the age-old illusion that it is possible to arrive at unimpeachable knowledge of material reality.

In *The Death of Nature*, Caroline Merchant laments the demise of a widely accepted idea of nature, but in her view it died some four centuries ago. The authentic, biologically grounded concept of an organic nature actually was supplanted, though perhaps only temporarily, by the mechanistic, male-oriented Newtonian-Cartesian philosophy that accompanied the seventeenth-century scientific revolution. The basic model for that philosophy was the machine, and it has

> permeated and reconstructed human consciousness so totally that today we scarcely question its validity. Nature, society, and

---

14. Fredric Jameson, *Postmodernism, or the Cultural Logic of Late Capitalism*, p. ix, Durham, NC: Duke University Press, 1991.

the human body are composed of interchangeable atomized parts that can be repaired or replaced from outside. The "technological fix" mends an ecological malfunction. . . . The mechanical view of nature now taught in most Western schools is accepted without question as our everyday, common sense reality. . . . The removal of animistic, organic assumptions about the cosmos constituted the death of nature.[15]

But Merchant leaves open the possibility of resurrecting and refining the premodern, organic idea of nature. Perhaps, she implies, the desperation induced by the accelerating ecological crisis will lead humankind to repudiate the mechanical view of nature and reaffirm a humane organicism.[16]

Among the prominent obituaries for the idea of nature, however, the most pertinent here is Bill McKibben's *The End of Nature*. He argues that nature came to an end, both as a discrete biophysical entity and as a meaningful concept, when Earth's atmospheric envelope was penetrated—and its filtering capacities damaged—by greenhouse gases and other manufactured chemicals.[17] By encompassing all of Earth's space, the expanding technological power of modern industrial societies has rid the planet of unaltered nature. The last remaining patches of pristine wilderness are now wrapped in a layer of man-made atmosphere. In McKibben's view, however, the most serious consequences of the degradation of material nature are intellectual. They are

15. Caroline Merchant, *The Death of Nature: Women, Ecology, and the Scientific Revolution*, p. 193, San Francisco: Harper, 1989.

16. Caroline Merchant, *Radical Ecology: The Search for a Livable World*, New York: Routledge, 1992.

17. Subsequent observations of global warming are widely accepted as confirming evidence of the man-made transformation of Earth's atmospheric envelope.

at once psychological, conceptual, and spiritual. What concerns him most is the impoverishment of the collective consciousness. "We have killed off nature," he writes, "that world entirely independent of us which was here before we arrived and which encircled and supported our human society." It is as if the real meaning of the age-old concept of nature had only become apparent at the moment our technological power had made it obsolete. We "have ended the thing that has defined . . . nature for us," he writes, "—its separation from human society."[18]

The importance McKibben assigns to the erasure of nature's separateness distinguishes *The End of Nature* from other laments about the disappearance of nature. To my knowledge, he is the only writer who attaches vital significance to this seldom noted, seemingly banal attribute of the received idea of nature.[19] But exactly why is the independence of nature so important? Why does he think that it matters so much? Although McKibben does not quite answer the question, he does provide a telling clue. "We have deprived nature of its independence," he writes, "and that is fatal to its meaning. Nature's independence is its meaning, without it there is nothing but us."[20] It is a poignant confession: without nature there is nothing but us. For McKibben, like many ardent environmentalists, nature is an essentially religious or metaphysical concept. As he uses the word, *nature* refers to the foundational character of the world. To continue serving as an effective repository of ultimate meaning, however, nature must retain its status as a separate, discrete entity. To

18. Bill McKibben, *The End of Nature*, pp. 64, 96, New York: Random House, 1989.

19. Raymond Williams calls attention to the idea of nature's separateness in "The Idea of Nature," in *Problems of Materialism and Culture*, pp. 67–85, London: Verso, 1980.

20. McKibben, op. cit., p. 58.

compromise its independence, as McKibben movingly testifies, is to expose its devotee to the acute pain of cosmic loneliness or—as some would have it—atheism.

The tenability of the idea of wilderness, the oldest and most popular American variant of the idea of nature, also was called into question at the end of the century. In a provocative 1995 essay, "The Trouble with Wilderness; or, Getting Back to the Wrong Nature," William Cronon, a leading environmental historian, precipitated a heated controversy by asserting that the popular imagery of a pristine American wilderness or "virgin land" embodies a racist or colonialist falsification of the historical record.[21] Cronon had established the empirical basis for this judgment in *Changes in the Land*, his seminal 1983 study of the transformation of the New England terrain, long before the arrival of Europeans, by the indigenous peoples of North America. But now, with his 1995 essay, he shocked many environmentalists, for whom the idea of the unsullied American wilderness was sacrosanct, by disclosing its covert implications. By the time of the alleged European "discovery" of the New World, he argues, there no longer was anything "natural" about it. Far from "being the one place on earth that stands apart from humanity," he writes, the American wilderness is "entirely the creation of the culture that holds it dear." Actually, the mythic image of a "virgin, uninhabited land" was an ideological weapon in the service of the European conquest of the Americas, and it was "especially cruel when seen from the perspective of the Indians who had once called that land home."

---

21. William Cronon, ed., *Uncommon Ground, Toward Reinventing Nature*, pp. 69–90, New York: W.W. Norton, 1995, and republished in the *New York Times Magazine*, August 13, 1995. For a comprehensive collection of the arguments, pro and con, see J. Baird Callicott and Michael P. Nelson, *The Great New Wilderness Debate*, Athens and London: University of Georgia Press, 1998.

And yet Cronon, an ardent environmentalist and outdoors-man, cannot bring himself to repudiate the idea of wilderness. To be sure, he clearly explains what makes it objectionable. "Any way of looking at nature that encourages us to believe that we are separate from nature—as wilderness tends to do—is likely," he concedes, "to reinforce environmentally irresponsible be-havior." But he also acknowledges that respect for wilderness entails respect for nonhuman forms of life. Like many environ-mentalists, in fact, he had responded to the prevalence of arro-gant anthropocentrism—especially the unfeeling disregard for the well-being of animals—by embracing a version of species egalitarianism. Now, seemingly contradicting himself, he con-cedes that the idea of the "autonomy of nonhuman nature . . . [may be] an indispensable corrective to human arrogance." He admits to being torn between his viewpoint as a scholar and as a committed environmentalist or, put differently, between his-torically informed skepticism about—and reverence for—the idea of wilderness. Cronon is unable, finally, to resolve his ambivalence. Like the pre-Darwinian idea of a separate nature, the idea of wilderness as a discrete entity proves to be irremedi-ably ambiguous and unstable.

In the event, however, Cronon proposes a way to circumvent the shortcomings of the idea. He recommends that environmen-talists follow the lead of their patron saints, Henry Thoreau and John Muir, and replace the idea of wilderness with the simpler, less problematic idea of wildness. (After founding the Sierra Club in 1892, Muir had chosen, as its official motto, Thoreau's fa-mous epigram: "In Wildness is the preservation of the World.") The great merit of wildness as a locus of value and meaning, he notes, is that unlike wilderness, it "can be found anywhere: in the seemingly tame fields and woodlots of Massachusetts, in the cracks of a Manhattan sidewalk, even in the cells of our own body." Whereas wilderness is a particular kind of place (one that

exhibits no signs of human intervention), wildness is an attribute
of living organisms that may turn up anywhere: a blue jay or a
daisy in a Manhattan park, he contends, is no less wild than its
counterpart in the Rocky Mountains. As might be expected,
Cronon's critics were quick to note something tenuous, even
quixotic, about this proposal. But granted that it is unlikely to
resolve the conflict about wilderness, it nonetheless calls attention to the critical shortcoming the idea of wilderness shares with
the idea of a separate nature. As Cronon warns, and as the devastation of the American wilderness attests, the belief that we
are separate from nature encourages what he all-too-gently calls
"environmentally irresponsible behavior."

The year 1970 was when the ecological crisis caught up with
the idea of nature. Public anxiety about the devastation of the
natural world had grown steadily in the aftermath of Hiroshima
and the onset of the nuclear arms race. But it was not until 1970,
the year of the first Earth Day, that the emerging environmental
movement exhibited its potential political power. In that year
the president proposed and the Congress enacted the National
Environmental Policy Act, the Clean Air Act, and the act establishing the Environmental Protection Agency. At roughly the
same time, moreover, it became evident that the word *environment* was supplanting the word *nature* in American public discourse. This was no coincidence. The two signal merits of the
idea of the environment, as compared with the idea of nature,
are its unequivocal materiality and inclusiveness. It refers to the
entire biophysical surround—or environ—we inhabit; it encom-
passes all that is built and unbuilt, artificial and natural, within
the terrain that surrounds us. As suggested by the closely associated verb, *to environ*, moreover, environments invariably are
products of human agency. All of which makes the idea of environment, in sharp contrast with the idea of nature, relatively

useless as a repository of abstract ideas—of moral, religious, or metaphysical meaning.

Thus it was the ecological crisis that finally and conclusively exposed the ambiguity and instability inherent in the age-old idea of a separate nature. For millennia, after all, nature so conceived had served as a valued, all-purpose embodiment of metaphysical abstractions. Nature had been depicted as the creation of God and the habitation of Satan, as harmonious and chaotic, beneficent and hostile, as something we must revere and something we had to conquer. To the inconvenience of practicing natural scientists, this rich deposit of meaning had become embedded in the common language. Ever since the seventeenth-century scientific revolution, they had been advocating linguistic reforms aimed at circumventing the imprecision and ambiguity created by figurative language. In a revealing passage of the *Origin of Species*, for example, Darwin feels compelled to defend himself for using "metaphorical expressions." But it is difficult, he confesses, "to avoid personifying the word Nature," and to elucidate he painstakingly offers a precise definition of the crucial word. "I mean by Nature," he writes, "only the aggregate action and product of many natural laws, and by laws the sequence of events as ascertained by us."[22]

Darwin's recourse to this abstract, featureless, ungraspable— if scientifically unobjectionable—definition was prophetic. It prefigured the eclipse of the idea of nature in our time. The very neutrality and blankness of the word *nature*, as Darwin defines it, anticipates the contemporary preference for the word *environment*. It is not hard to understand why this matter-of-fact word seems preferable, for example, to scientific ecologists, legislators, political activists, officials of the Environmental Protection

---

22. Darwin, op. cit., p. 88.

Agency, or, for that matter, anyone attempting to cope, in one way or another, with the the practical, matter-of-fact problems of air and water pollution, resource depletion, species extinction, and global warming. Yet there is a supreme irony in all this. What now has proven to be a fatal shortcoming of the idea of a separate nature in America—its limitless hospitality to moral, religious, and metaphysical meanings—had for centuries been the reason for its well-nigh universal appeal.

But in recent years several ecologically oriented writers, including William Cronon, have endorsed a reform, at once conceptual and linguistic, aimed at salvaging the venerable idea of nature.[23] They propose to rehabilitate the philosophically nuanced distinction, favored by Hegel and Marx, between *first nature* and *second nature*. In this usage, first nature is the original nonhuman world (it presumably embraces the entire cosmos) as it existed before the evolution of *Homo sapiens*, and second nature is the artificial—material and cultural—environment that humanity later superimposed upon first nature. On this view, manifestly, nature is all. Unlike the traditional idea of a separate nature, the first nature/second nature distinction is consonant with the received history of nature, and especially with the centrality, in that history, of the process of biological evolution and the emergence of life on Earth. During all but the final minutes, as it were, of this distilled historical narrative, first nature was all.

But then, beginning with the emergence of life and, eventually, *Homo sapiens*, the encroachment of second nature transformed the surface of the planet. To be sure, we know that every organism modifies its habitat in some degree, but the extent of

---

23. William Cronon, *Nature's Metropolis: Chicago and the Great West*, p. xviiff, New York: W.W. Norton, 1991; Janet Biehl, *Rethinking Ecofeminist Politics*, pp. 117–118, South End Press, 1991.

humanity's modification of Earth exceeds that of other species by orders of magnitude. Second nature is chiefly a human creation, and in recent centuries the rapidly accelerating expansion of its power and its territorial scope has had a devastating impact on global ecosystems. The result is a grave crisis in the relations, or putative balance, between first and second nature. A singular value of the two natures distinction is the clarity it affords in characterizing the brief, limited, but unique role of humanity in the overall history of nature. Because the resulting narrative is divided into two distinct phases—before and after the emergence of life—it does full justice to humanity's unmatched power to create a unique material and cultural environment. At the same time, however, the distinction has the inestimable merit of retaining the conception of a single, subdivided yet fundamentally unified realm of nature.

from the *Arab World*

# THE CONCEPTIONS OF NATURE
# IN ARABIC THOUGHT

———

Nader El-Bizri

## ETYMOLOGICAL REFLECTIONS

**THE CLASSICAL ARABIC CONCEPTIONS** of nature as *tab'* or *tabi'a*, which are manifest in variegated methods of reasoning and praxis, were partly influenced by the Ancient Greek accounts of nature as *phusis*, and they partially resembled the Latin meditations on *natura*, while being additionally shaped by monotheistic religious and etymological directives.

The abstract expression *tabi'a*, which is the standard Arabic lexical unit that corresponds with the Ancient Greek "*phusis*" and its Latin correlate "*natura*," derives from the root term *tab'*. In prephilosophical usage, the term *tabi'a* was not common, and we rather encounter in the Arabic language expressions like *taba'a* and *tab'* that designate the act of "sealing," "stamping," "branding," or the "making of an impression or imprint."[1] While the

---

1. For instance, the expression *taba'a*, from the root *tab'*, is used in the Qur'anic context in the sense of sealing something by way of blocking it. That God hath sealed (*taba'a*) the hearts of infidels and unbelievers as well as stamped locked

common use of the term tab' denotes the workings of character, temperamental disposition, or inherent constitutional
propensity, the word tabi'a was coined for the purposes of
philosophical enunciation to refer to the self-expression of
nature according to which beings let themselves be revealed
as they are.[2] Consequently, when we use the terms tabi'a or tab',
we denote what is inherent in the identity of things as what
belongs to their essence/quiddity.[3] In this sense, these lexical
designators become intellectually attributed to an essentialist elucidation of the beingness of beings in the manner that
they hint of the aptitudes that drive the comportment of individuals, as well as point to the susceptibility of things to
undertake a certain course of movement. Moreover, from a religious standpoint, the term tabi'a was subsequently used to refer
to adaptations that are impressed on things upon their creation,
hence designating the eschatological state of being created with

(taba'a) their sight and hearing (Qur'an, 9:93; 16:108; 47:16; 7:100; 40:35;
10:74; 9:78; 63:3).

2. Muhsin S. Mahdi, Alfarabi and the Foundation of Islamic Political Philosophy, pp. 23–
24, Chicago: University of Chicago Press, 2001, with a foreword by Charles
E. Butterworth, hereinafter Alfarabi. Refer also to D. E. Pingree and S. Nomanul
Haq, "Tabi'a," in The Encyclopaedia of Islam, Vol. 10, pp. 25–28, eds. P. J. Bearman,
Th. Binaquis, C. E. Bosworth, E. van Donzel, W. P. Heinrichs, Leiden: Brill,
2000; Seyyed Hossein Nasr, An Introduction to Islamic Cosmological Doctrines: Concep-
tions of Nature and Methods Used for Its Study by Ikhwan al-Safa', al-Biruni and Ibn Sina,
London: Thames and Hudson, 1978.

3. Like its Arabic counterpart, the Latin word natura, which is derived from
the root nasci (namely: "to be born" or "to originate"), with its associated term
natus (that is "born" or "originated"), ultimately designates "that which lets
something originate from itself." The Greek phusis was also classically investi-
gated in relation to the expression phuo: as begetting or letting come into being, wherein nature points to the acts of generation. For further particulars,
see Martin Heidegger, "On the Essence and Concept of Phusis in Aristotle's Physics
Beta I," trans. William McNeill, in Pathmarks (Wegmarken), p. 183, ed. William
McNeill, Cambridge: Cambridge University Press, 1998.

the predisposition to serve particular purposes and realize a certain destiny.

In the *Book of Definitions* (*Kitab al-hudud*), Avicenna (Ibn Sina; d. 1037 C.E.) draws a subtle distinction between *tab'* and *tabi'a*. In his view, nature as *tab'* is a disposition by virtue of which a species achieves its completeness, and it is thus more general than nature as *tabi'a*. Nature as *tab'* thus refers to a generic disposition, while nature as *tabi'a* applies to the particulars of individuals, as well as acts as the essential first principle behind the motion and rest of that in which it inheres, and is thusly the source of its alteration or permanence.[4] As a physician and philosopher, Avicenna also took *tabi'a* to be indicative of temperament as well as designating the four humors and the temperature of bodies.[5]

The claim that construes *tabi'a* as being the cause of motion and rest of that in which it is present in essence rather than in accident is derived from Aristotle's *Physics*.[6] For, it is said therein that nature as *phusis* is the principle and the cause of being moved or of being at rest in the thing in which it belongs primarily and in virtue of that thing, but not accidentally.[7] Aristotle's conception of *phusis* is furthermore identified with the form and matter of composite physical bodies, while

---

4. Avicenna, *Kitab al-hudud* (*Livre des définitions*), section 13, p. 22 Arabic text, p. 33 French translation, trans. Amélie Marie Goichon, Cairo: Institut Français d'Archéologie Orientale du Caire, 1963.

5. Ibid., section 12, pp. 21–22 Arabic text, pp. 31–33 French translation. Avicenna's definitions of *tab'* and *tabi'a* are herein akin to what we encounter in Aristotle's *Physics*, 192b13–14, 192b35–37, 193a10, 193a28–30. See Aristotle, *Physics*, ed. W. D. Ross, Oxford: Oxford University Press, 1950.

6. Aristotle, *Physics*, op. cit., 192b20–23.

7. It must be noted here that Aristotle's *Physics* is a tract that investigates the nature of motion and rest and their principles, be it in the shape of locomotion, increase and decrease, or as a general alteration and change (*Physics*, op. cit., 201a10–11).

also defined in terms of essence/substance (*ousia*) and the categories (such as when talking about the nature of a triangle).[8] Herein, nature gets associated with knowledge, given that it pertains to the essence of things, and to the causal nexus due to which they get manifested in actuality. After all, the association of certain causes with their corresponding effects permits us to offer explanations regarding the circumstances that surround the nature of something. The appeal to nature also warrants our causal justification of knowledge, as well as grounds our proclaimed rational modes of understanding, including the generalizations we posit regarding the purported laws that govern the universe.

When thinking about the refraction of etymology within the complex modes of intellection, the Greek conception of nature as *phusis* is not readily transferable into a Roman/Latin idea of *natura*, nor is it simply transformable into an Arabic notion of *tabi'a*. After all, some metaphysical adjustment is at play when we shift from the pagan classical accounts of the cosmos to monotheistic grasps of creation. This observation also applies to the subsequent early modern European explanation of nature as a mechanistic model of machination, which differs in scope from the precedent historical cosmological paragons (be they Greek, Arabic, or Latin). The realm of *phusis* was taken to be that of the immortals that surged from nothingness at the beginnings of time in Greek cosmology, thus lying beside the likes of *khaos*, *khronos*, or *eros*. *Phusis* was also conceived as *ousia*, namely "being" that is grasped by the Latin scholarship as *substantia/essentia*, which is the origin of motion and rest. This essence of nature as *ousia* is said to be understood by the Greeks as a stable presencing that is a mode of coming forth into the unhidden (Greek *parousia*),

---

8. Ibid., 192b8–193b21. Moreover, by the categories, we mean time, place, quality, quantity, relation, etc.

which is not a mere presentness or an objective presence.[9] Herein, the Latin *natura* and the Arabic *tabi'a* do not readily convey what their Greek counterpart *phusis* originally meant, namely, the state of affairs of things in the course of growing, producing, and bearing fruit, each according to its unique quality.

The Greek conception of nature essentially refers to the teleological end toward which something tends in its existence.[10] For instance, the nature of a boy is to grow into a man, and the nature of an acorn is to grow into an oak. Nature is hence causal, and, specifically, teleological, wherein things are subject to a continual motion due to their nature by virtue of which they tend to achieve their proper completeness in meeting their end. In view of this, Aristotle furthermore insinuated that truth is entangled with being, in the sense that *phusis* is intrinsically *aletheia*, namely, that nature is the unconcealment of what is concealed as it is implied in truth. And it is in this sense that his *Physics*, which impacted the unfolding of the Arabic peripatetic tradition, is to be interpreted as the ontology of nature, wherein seeing and direct intuitive perception act as the principal modes by which we attend to the truth of being.[11]

From a Syrian and Greek stoic perspective, which found its way to Arabic systems of thought, nature as *phusis* connoted a living and conscious growing of all beings that was consistent

---

9. It might be said that the *logos* contributes herein to the gathering into the unhidden of presencing by way of letting beings be unconcealed in their self-showing. See Heidegger, op. cit., pp. 203, 206–208, 213–215.

10. Based on Aristotle's book IV of the *Physics*, it is said that it is of the nature of things to go back to the proper place (*topos*) to which they belong, namely, that heavy bodies travel downward toward the earth, and that light bodies travel upward toward the heavens.

11. See Martin Heidegger, *Sein und Zeit*, *Gesamtausgabe Band* 2, sections 36, 44, Tübingen: Max Niemeyer, 1977.

with their intrinsic character as the modes of the outflowing
of the divine cosmic order. Consequently, the talk about nature principally hinted at the workings of a creator or an arti-
san demiurge, whose natural rules operatively and willfully
govern all creatures. In this cosmic picture, all things are seen
as harmoniously part of the whole qua nature, which is thusly
construed as akin to divine providence and destiny in the manner it moves matter and pervades all beings by bringing them
into interconnectedness. For, unlike the neoplatonists who associated nature with the material "fallen" realm, and thus
construed it as being the lowest and weakest sphere in the emanation scheme, the stoics identified nature with divinity. Despite this distinction, both schools of classical thought (stoicism
and neoplatonism) had numerous followers among the Arab
medieval philosophers.[12]

## SKEPTICISM

The influence of Aristotle's conception of nature, as the cause
or first principle of motion and rest, was not restricted to the
literature of the peripatetic Arab philosophers but was also
shared by some Muslim theologians by way of an assimilative
dialectical negation. This matter may be partly affirmed by what
is advanced by Abu Hamid al-Ghazali (Algazel, d. 1111 c.e.)
in his critical tract, *The Incoherence of the Philosophers*, in which he

---

12. The origin of the neoplatonic influence in Arabic thought may be attributed to the tradition of the *Liber de causis* (known in Arabic as *Kitab al-khayr
al-mahd: The Book of Pure Goodness*) and the *Theologia Aristotelis* (a tract attributed
to Porphyry, which was erroneously assimilated to Aristotle's corpus). Regarding the subtle stoic influences in the history of Arabic thought, see Fehmi
Jedaane, *L'Influence du Stoïcisme sur la Pensé Musulmane*, Beirut: Dar al-machreq,
1967.

intricately imparted the conception of nature with a hermeneutic turn that depicted *tabi'a* as akin to the notion of *'ada* as custom, habit, or convention, whose continuity is warranted by divine providence.[13] His views were founded on the classical refutation of causality by the exponents of *kalam* (dialectical theology) in their account of natural phenomena. In contrast with the philosophers, al-Ghazali did not believe that nature was ordered by way of a causal nexus. Yet, in denying causation, the idea of natural science seems to be hardly plausible, and the ontological significance of *tabi'a* appears groundless. Under these peculiar circumstances, prediction and inference can barely be pronounced and the realm of the possible becomes open to uncanny happenings that unsettle our profound sense of concrete familiarity.

Following Aristotle, philosophers like Alfarabi (Abu Nasr al-Farabi; Alpharabius, d. 950 c.e.), Avicenna (Ibn Sina, d. 1037 c.e.), and Averroes (Ibn Rushd, d. 1198 c.e.) conceived nature as a plenum that consists of a continuum of beings who are interconnected by causality and determined by presencing and permanence. On his part, al-Ghazali poignantly rejected their naturalist picturing of the world by way of positing divine volition as the cause of all created beings. He argued that while inanimate creatures have no power at all, animate beings have a derivative power that is imparted to them by the creator through a simultaneity that excludes causal efficiency. He consequently held that what is usually referred to as a cause along with what is taken to be its effect are occurrences created with the semblance of being generated via necessary connections.

Al-Ghazali stated in the seventeenth tract of his *Incoherence of the Philosophers* that "the connection between what is habitually

---

13. Mahdi, *Alfarabi*, op. cit., p. 24.

believed to be a cause and what is habitually believed to be an effect is not necessary."[14] He also added that this apparent connection is due to a prior divine decree that creates the seeming cause and its effect as being contiguous. As he further argued, the burning of the cotton when in contact with fire does not readily entail that the latter is the natural agent for the flaming of the former. For al-Ghazali proclaimed that it is indeed possible that the cotton gets in contact with fire without burning, or that the cotton gets transmuted into burnt ashes without having been in contact with fire. In denying the causal connection between the cotton meeting the fire and its consequent flaming, al-Ghazali asserted that God generates the accidental burning.

Al-Ghazali polemically asserted that observation does not warrant the causal principle, arguing that the power by virtue of which one object produces another is not discoverable from the essence or idea of either of these objects, and that the same applies to classes of events that generate one another.[15] In his view, we know about causation only from experience, given that the matters pertaining to causation are synthetic and empirical rather than determined by a priori propositions. The connection between what is habitually taken to be a cause and what is consequently taken to be its effect is thus not a logical relation, nor is it a link due to essence, but rather is an experiential association by way of custom. The inference concerning the connection between a cause and its effect is not necessary, or a priori, but is rather derived from observation, whereby this apparent and

14. Abu Hamid al-Ghazali, The Incoherence of the Philosophers (Tahafut al-falasifa), pp. 170–171, translation with introduction and notes by Michael Marmura, Provo, UT: Brigham Young University Press, 1997.

15. This line of reasoning found later echoes in David Hume's (d. 1776) skepticism with regard to causation and induction as set out in his Treatise on Human Nature.

frequent conjunction is based on a habit of association due to past experience.[16]

In al-Ghazali's view, observation allows us only to attest that an ignition occurs at the time the cotton is in contact with the fire. Yet, this state of affairs does not necessarily mean that the cotton is set ablaze due to the flaming agency of fire. Being conjunctive with something, being alongside it or merely in contact with it, does not entail that a necessary connection binds these contiguous phenomena or classes of events. Existing in apposition with something does not prove that what is as such exists by or due to what is near it. The burning occurring with and alongside the observed contact of the cotton with the fire does not mean that it occurs by or due to the fire. For all we see is that, at the time of the burning, the cotton is in contact with the fire. Moreover, the mere repetitiveness of this event of burning does not necessarily secure its future occurrence. Although the recurrence of this occasion might have the semblance of fixity and regularity that is usually attributed to causality, it is rather the continual custom in attesting to this repeated event that unshakably fixes in our minds the belief in natural causation and its assumed necessary connection between cause and effect. Consequently, and based on al-Ghazali's view, nature seems to be following a habitual course rather than a necessary one. His

16. This empirically determined account of causation is advanced by al-Ghazali in defense of monotheism, while being used by Hume in view of undermining religious belief altogether. The question of natural causation was readdressed in Immanuel Kant's (d. 1804) Kritik der Reinen Vernunft (Critique of Pure Reason) in defense of the principium causalitatis, wherein he argued that nature in an empirical sense constitutes a connection of appearances that follow necessary laws (Kritik, A216/B263). He also held that "nature" formaliter signified the connection of the determinations of a thing according to an inner rule of causality, while "nature" materialiter designated the sum of appearances insofar as they stand in interconnection due to an immanent principle of causation (Kritik, B446).

conception of nature thus gives expression to a form of theological occasionalism that opposes philosophical determinism[17]; herein, custom is contrasted with necessity whereby nature becomes unpredictable. The cement of the world, this causal connection that binds beings together, is thus almost cleared away. A vacuum henceforth pierces the plenum, and sets of possible worlds are in contest with the actual and concrete reality that is thinly grounded in our deeply entrenched habits.[18] Nature does then seem to be a gaping openness rather than an ordered closure, and our habitual reality is thus challenged in its apparent consistency and familiar coherence.

Al-Ghazali's skepticism was proposed in defense of the articles of faith and in upholding a theological belief in the occurrence of miracles as well as in confirming the possibility of resurrection. As a committed devout, he confirmed his belief that Abraham was thrown unto the fire without burning (Qur'an 21:69) and that God spoke to Moses (Qur'an 20:12–16) or that Jesus uttered in his cradle (Qur'an 3:45–46; 19:29–34). He moreover upheld the conviction that God lets the living rise from the dead and the dead surge from the living (Qur'an 3:27, 30:19). Henceforth, he affirmed the immortality of the soul, which optimistically confirms the soteriological idea of the afterlife as opposed to vain perdition.[19] Based

---

17. For instance, an occasionalist like Nicolas de Malebranche (d. 1715) argues that if only bodies and minds exist, and if bodies do not cause motion, then minds may be said to be the causal movers of things; however, being finite, minds cannot cause motion; therefore, only the perfectly infinite can causally be the prime mover.

18. The tragic maneuver of the skeptic herein indeed contentiously teases our impressionable imagination and defies our epistemological insecurity. The assailant of philosophical systems may thus not hesitate to wonder with a pessimist demeanor: "So, will the sun rise tomorrow?"

19. References to resurrection are abundant in the Qur'an: 16:38–40; 17:49–52; 19:66–72; 22:5–7; 50:3, 20–22, 41–44; 75:1–15; 79:10–12; 86:5–8.

on his line of thinking, the enframed nature becomes a vastness that is ubiquitously filled with God's signs (ayat), wherein all beings in the heavens and earth declare praises to His creation (Qur'an 24:41; 50:6–11). Nonetheless, miracles, as eventful anomalies, may still be seen within this outlook as "natural" aberrations rather than strictly preternatural, provided that we do not construe nature as regulated by necessary causal networks and rather think of it as determined by deviant habits. The miraculously uncanny is thus part of the natural course of things, though not following the patterns that we have been habitually familiarized with. Nature is hence not ordinary, but rather is extraordinary, and from a religious perspective, miracles accordingly occur within possible worlds, albeit not within the apparent environment of our entrenched collective custom. The realm of possibility may thus extend as far as the stretches of fictional imagining, and it is bound only by logic, for all is plausibly realizable by divinity unless it is termed by its grace as logically impossible.[20]

## NATURAL CAUSATION

It is believed that Averroes's treatise on the harmony between religion and philosophy, known as *Fasl al-maqal* (*The Decisive*

---

20. Al-Ghazali, op. cit., pp. 174, 179. According to the exponents of *kalam*, the realm of plausibility (or what is referred to in Arabic as *tajwiz*) is enclosed by logic. For example, it is possible that a chair gets transmuted into a table, but it is not possible that the circle gets squared. It is also impossible to affirm something and negate it simultaneously. This classic idea had its roots in the influence that the Imam Abu'l-Hasan al-Ash'ari (d. 935 c.e.) had on al-Ghazali's formative thinking. See Abu'l-Hasan al-Ash'ari, *Maqalat al-islamiyyin*, ed. Muhammad Muhyi al-Din 'Abd al-Hamid, Cairo: Maktabat al-nahda al-misriyya, 1969.

Treatise), was written in defense of philosophy against the views of opponents influenced by al-Ghazali's thought and by ash'arite kalam (dialectical theology). It is also said that Averroes was trying therein to furnish a legal retort to the condemnation of philosophical thinking by the followers of al-Ghazali's line and its theological imports. Moreover, the very drafting of Fasl al-maqal may have been indicative of the prevalent unpopularity of peripatetic philosophy in Averroes's intellectual milieu.[21] Nonetheless, al-Ghazali's critique of the philosophers, particularly of Alfarabi and Avicenna, as set in The Incoherence of the Philosophers, was directly interrogated by Averroes in another dense critical tract entitled The Incoherence of the Incoherence.[22] Al-Ghazali's doubts concerning the necessary connection between a cause and its effect were radically challenged by Averroes, who vehemently argued that the refutation of observed sensible causal links, and their conceptual substitution with habits, is an irrational exercise in sophistry that ultimately leads to the denial of the nature of things, wherein definitions become abhorrently implausible, and the determined properties of trait become unsubstantiated.[23] Averroes was also not sure about what is meant by al-Ghazali's use of the term 'ada (habit or custom) in the context of talking about the habitual character of causes and effects. For Averroes wondered whether habit was therein attributable to the agent of the eventful act (namely to God), or whether it was due to beings themselves, or to those who judge what is habitually grasped as a causal connection. Averroes then affirmed that conversing about habits is not to be attributed to the eternal God

21. Averroes, On the Harmony of Philosophy and Religion (Fasl al-maqal), 3rd reprint, p. 17, trans. George Hourani, London: Luzac, 1976.

22. Averroes, Tahafut al-tahafut (The Incoherence of the Incoherence), pp. 505–509, ed. Muhammad 'Abid al-Jabiri, Beirut: Markaz dirasat al-wihda al-'arabiyya, 1998.

23. Ibid., p. 518.

since it implies an inadmissible change in the divine agency. As for the claim that habits are associated with phenomenal creatures, he adds that only animate beings follow habitual patterns, and that these are in turn attributable to their proper natures. He consequently concluded that habits do get assimilated to nature, and he furthermore asserted that the association of habits with our modes of judging phenomena is derived from our human nature. In this line of interrogation, Averroes thus questioned the ambivalence of al-Ghazali's equivocal use of the term habit to designate what is usually attributed to nature, hence seeing the substitution of nature with habit as misleading and redundant.[24]

Based on "possible-world semantics," volitional divine intervention may break the cycle of habit by creating something out of nothing, transforming a being into another, turning an inanimate being animate, or resurrecting the dead.[25] The realm of the actual world is thus plausibly extendable beyond the concreteness of our physical sensibility. Averroes for his part regarded such unjustifiable imaginings as naturally implausible. For what al-Ghazali pictured as an epistemological habitual regularity in the way we inductively account for phenomena was considered by Averroes as the ordering causal principle of the cosmos.

For a religious mind, the very eventuality of the uncanny confronts us with a sense of groundlessness that disrupts the confidence derived from the familiarities that lie at the root of our thinking. The religious space in which Abraham gets thrown

---

24. Averroes's bent in reasoning accords here with what we encounter in Aristotle's account of habit as hexis, namely, as a disposition that is very hard to displace whether acquired or natural. See Aristotle, Metaphysics, 1022b4–14, ed. W. D. Ross, Oxford: Clarendon Press, 1997.

25. Averroes, Tahafut al-tahafut, op. cit., pp. 511–512.

into the fire without burning is that of a possible world that is indeed at odds with what divine compassion has mercifully led us to believe is the sole concrete reality. While al-Ghazali strenuously attempts to account for this unusual Abrahamic environment, Averroes shows reverence to the articles of faith by elegantly knowing where explanations come to an end. It is after all a grave philosophical dilemma for figures like al-Ghazali or Averroes to know how to stand in humility in view of solemnly receiving the verse "We said, 'O fire! Be thou cold and safe on Abraham!'" (Qur'an 21:69).

Although al-Ghazali's universe is marked by a mytho-poetic sense of wonder, it was nonetheless grounded in the intricate atomist physics of the theologians, which competitively contrasted the Aristotelian physics that inspired the diction of most Arab philosophers.[26] Based on the physical theories of kalam, on which al-Ghazali's speculations are founded, substances are none other than atoms (atomos) that constitute the smallest indivisible particles and discrete entities that cannot be partitioned. These building blocks of the universe get joined together by way of accident, not essence, in multiple minuscule geometrical formations and articulations. In their gatherings, they retain enclosed voids between them as well as in the vaster regions of being that surround them. Unlike the cosmos of Aristotelians, which was determined as a plenum, the universe of the exponents of kalam affirms the existential reality of the vacuum, while also conceiving of time as a processional structure that admits temporal leaps rather than being a mere passing continuum. The atomist time space thus allows for the rearticulation of existing corporeal formations whereby new atomic recollections permit the trans-

---

26. Regarding an informative account of the atomist theories of kalam, see Alnoor Dhanani, *The Physical Theory of Kalam: Atoms, Space, and Void in Basrian Mu'tazili Cosmology*, Leiden: Brill, 1994.

ference of constitutional shapes from one object to another, granted that the atomic accidents of taste, smell, weight, texture, heat, and solidity also get modified in this extraordinary displacement. Having this physical theory in mind, we may fairly say that Averroes hastily degraded the merits of al-Ghazali's ontotheological speculations by associating the latter's skepticism with irrationality or derogatory forms of sophistry.[27] For although the passionate narrative of the mythos carries an internal coherence (despite some of its occasional logical ambiguities), it is regrettably often misjudged by the logos as marked by fallacy.[28]

Even though Averroes may have been the most prominent of the philosophers in responding to al-Ghazali's skepticism, the dispute over causation and nature remained an unsettled quandary in the course of development of Arabic thought. It is indeed remarkable that among the religious authorities themselves we notice an emergent penchant in accepting a talk about causation and nature independently of habit. This may have been attested to in the works of the influential Imam Ahmad Ibn Taymiyya (d. ca. 1328 C.E.), as well as in the works of 'Abdu'l-Rahman Ibn Ahmad al-Iji (d. 1355 C.E.) and 'Ali Bin Muhammad al-Jurjani (d. 1413 C.E.).[29] Moreover, thinkers like Ibn Hazm (d. 1064 C.E.) and Avempace (Ibn Bajja, d. 1138 C.E.)

---

27. This line of thinking is reminiscent of what we encounter with the atomism of Pierre Gassendi (d. 1655), who attempted to revive the doctrines of Lucretius and Epicurus in view of advancing a solid critique of Aristotle and the Cartesian system. This matter is notably evident in his *Disquisitio Metaphysica* (ca. 1644), and it is equally emphasized in his objections and replies to the *Meditationes de prima philosophia* (ca. 1641) of René Descartes (d. 1650).

28. Namely, what a logician would consider to be the falsity of a *petitio principii*.

29. For further particulars, see Muhammad 'Abid al-Jabiri, *Bunyat al-'aql al-'arabi*, 5th printing, Beirut: Markaz dirasat al-wihda al-'arabiyya, 1996; George Tarabishi, *Ishkaliyyat al-'aql al-'arabi*, Beirut: Dar al-saqi, 1998.

were also resolutely opposed to the physics of *kalam* and to its
implied doubts concerning the causal conceptions of *tab'* and
*tabi'a*.[30] Moses Maimonides (Musa Ibn Maymun, d. 1204 C.E.)
was equally solicitous in his examination of the theologians' bent
on refuting the notion of *tab'* in their strenuous attempts to
demonstrate that divine volition creates accidents in substances
without the mediation of a causal nature.[31] Furthermore, the
distinguished historian 'Abdu'l-Rahman Ibn Muhammad Ibn
Khaldun (d. 1395 C.E.) questioned the theologians' use of logic
in their attempt to show how the opinions derived from physics, with their metaphysical basis, were simply applicable to these
arts only without affecting the articles of faith.[32]

## ONTOLOGY

According to Alfarabi, the subject matter of natural science is
that of natural bodies insofar as these are akin to artificial bodies in their unconcealed perceptual qualities or in their veiled

---

30. Ibn Bajja, *Sharh al-sama' al-tabi'i*, ed. Ma'n Ziadeh, Beirut: Dar al-kindi, 1978;
Ibn Hazm, *al-Fasl fi al-milal wa'l-ahwa' wa'l-nihal*, Vol. I–II, Cairo: 1899, 1903.
31. Musa Ibn Maymun, *Dalalat al-ha'irin*, p. 205, ed. Hasan Atay, Anqara, Tur-
key: Anqara University, 1974; Moses Maimonides, *The Guide for the Perplexed*, trans.
M. Friedländer, New York: Dover, 1956.
32. Ibn Khaldun also believed that the intellectual cum rational sciences are
natural to all human beings inasmuch as we are thinking beings. Of these
philosophical sciences, he listed the classical seven areas in the classification
order: beginning with logic, followed by mathematics (arithmetic, geometry
[inclusive of optics], astronomy, music), physics (with medicine as one of its
subdivisions), then finally crowning the system with metaphysics. See Ibn
Khaldun, *The Muqaddimah, An Introduction to History*, 9th paperback print, pp. 352,
371–373, 385–386, 389, trans. Franz Rosenthal, ed. and abridged by N. J.
Dawood, Princeton, NJ, New York: Princeton University Press, Bollingen Foundation, 1989.

governing principles.[33] Nature, moreover, is grasped by him as a process of making that is guided by divine design and intent, whose radically degraded counterparts are attested to in the crafts generated in expression of our human will. However, this does not mean that he simply took natural science, which is a theoretical cognitive inquest besides mathematics and logic, to be readily assimilated to practical arts or vocations. Rather, he believed that natural science finds its highest theoretical determination in metaphysics, which inquires about beings and the ultimate principles of their reality by way of attending to the question of being in view of the workings of divinity.

The leverage attested to in the move from physics qua natural science to metaphysics qua divine science is mediated by a shift in emphasis from an ontic investigation of things to an ontological speculation about the condition of their being. However, although the questions of physics lead the inquirer to metaphysics, the classificatory and cognitive distinction between both disciplines remains clearly delineated. Nonetheless, from an ontological perspective, and following the Greek sources, metaphysics was seen as a form of physics qua epistemic *phusike*, namely, a mode of knowing *phusis*.[34] Herein, motion was axial to meta-physical cum physical inquiries; hence investigating *phusis* was a mode of seeking to grasp the ordering stability in the presencing of the beingness of beings. After all, the investigation of motion, which is the subject matter of classical physics, leads to a metaphysical inquiry about the First Unmoved Mover, who is beyond extension and corporeal existence.[35] As

33. Mahdi, *Alfarabi*, op. cit., pp. 78–79.

34. Heidegger, "On the Essence and Concept of *Phusis* in Aristotle's *Physics Beta* I," op. cit., p. 185.

35. See, for instance, Aristotle's *Physics*, op. cit., Book VIII, Chapter 5.

a study of nature, physics thus also sustains questions that are ontotheological in character. Based on this outlook, the Ancient Greeks and the Arabs were metaphysically readied to gracefully submit to a natural order of things that is warranted by divine providence, and sporadically threatened by its wrath.

If nature constitutes the existential totality of observable and measurable worldly phenomena, then thinking about nature is ultimately an ontological endeavor as much as it is also an ontic mode of investigating the physical world. Consequently, the question concerning the essence/quiddity of nature is entangled with that of the meaning of being. For instance, the Arab neoplatonists saw nature as a whole that is generated by way of an emanation form of creation that is articulated along "a great chain of being." Natural beings were thus grasped as creatures that essentially belong to the sublunar realm, which is marked by the refraction of forms in matter as attested to with composite bodily modes of existing. However, one cannot simply talk about nature per se within this cosmological system, given that what pertains to nature is none other than a gradational ontological station in the participation in being. Having noted that, one could still talk about the whole emanationist outlook as a mode of naturalizing creation, given that it is principally governed by a causal principle, wherein divine effusion pertains to the nature of the one. For all that issues-out-forth from the one is determined by the ontological granting of its nature, which lets all that is effused receive the gift of participating in it. This optimistic picturing of being, which suffers from the melancholy of separation from the source, has had many adherents in the history of Islamic thought. Among others, thinkers such as Alfarabi, Avicenna, Muhyi al-Din Ibn ʿArabi (d. 1240 C.E.), Shihab al-Din Yahya Suhrawardi (d. 1191 C.E.), Nasir al-Din Tusi (d. 1274 C.E.), and Mulla Sadra (d. 1641 C.E.), were each impacted in his own way by this neoplatonic ontology. Within this

lineage in thinking, cosmology became oriented by the granting nature of divine goodness, whose emanation is modulated
along a series of hierarchical causation. This cosmic image continued to be at work within what subsequently developed into a
mature form of natural philosophy, which was initially questioned by many theologians in the name of preserving a sense
of the miraculous, even if this meant that the confidence in the
concreteness of the physical reality had to be compromised.

Thinking about nature is ontologically determined by the
manner in which the beingness of beings comes to be. The eventuality of being is herein linked to the manner by which the generation of all creatures is brought forth by divine command, for
were not believers enigmatically summoned: "But His command, when He intendeth a thing, is only that He saith unto it:
'Be!' and it is. . . . When He decreeth a matter, He saith unto it:
'Be!' and it is" (Qur'an, 6:73; 16:40; 19:35; 36:82; 40:68)? This
uncanny creative utterance is also attested to in the manner that
Adam and Jesus were created out of dust by the sacral command:
"Be!" (Qur'an, 3:59). With this scripture in view, one is perhaps
theologically inclined to say that the believers were enticed to
demonstrate without impunity their departure from pagan conceptions of nature, including the Greek traditions.[36] After all, the
Ancient Greeks saw *phusis* as an unalterable preexistent principle
that regulates generation and corruption, while most of the let-
tered doctors of Islam did not separate the study of nature from
a close and continual attending to the question of divinity. Their
religiously motivated contemplation of nature and its workings
was thus seen as an inevitable undertaking on the fatiguing

36. Meaning by this the *peri phuseos* tradition of the likes of Anaximander (ca.
610–546 B.C.), Anaxagoras (ca. 500–428 B.C.), Parmenides of Elea (b. 510 B.C.),
Heraclitus of Ephesus (b. 535 B.C.), Empedocles of Acragas (fl. 450 B.C.), or
Epicurus (ca. 341–271 B.C.).

pathways of spiritual journeying, in addition to associating this reflective task with scientific pursuits.[37]

One of the principal popularized accounts of nature in the classical Arabic traditions in science and philosophy is encountered in *The Epistles of the Brethren of Purity (Rasa'il Ikhwan al-Safa')*.[38] In the sixth tract of the physical cum natural sciences part of this encyclopedic compendium, the Brethren of Purity (Ikhwan al-Safa', the anonymous members of an Iraqi fraternity, ca. tenth century C.E.) offer some pointers regarding what they take to be the quiddity/essence of nature. Therein, they hold that nature (*tabi'a*) is the power/potency of the universal cosmic soul that is prevalently at work in all beings. Following Aristotle, they moreover posited nature as the principle of motion and rest of all creatures, as well as taking it to be the origin of the teleological unfolding of generation, growth, and corruption. The universal cosmic soul was seen by them as the spirit of the world that acts as the efficient existential cause that generates nature. Unlike the human artifice, which derives its materials from what is other than itself, the products of nature are self-made. Hence, minerals qua inorganic entities, as well as plants and animals, together with their divisions according to kinds, genera, species, classes, and individuals, all were seen by the Brethren as the resulting effects of the universal soul, which mediates its causal power through nature's productivity. In this view, the semblance of corporeal permanence and physical presencing of composite natural bodies is existentially derived from this cosmic source. The causal chain that regulates nature is determined by the actions of the celestial spheres, which are self-same in their

---

37. As some theologians might have held, the recorded scriptural Qur'an (*tadwini*) corresponds with the universe insofar as this latter is seen as the Qur'an of creative generation (*takwini*).

38. Ikhwan al-Safa', *Rasa'il Ikhwan al-Safa'*, ed. Butrus Bustani, Beirut: Sadir, 1957.

perennial existence and their circular motions, as opposed to the temporal nature of the sublunar beings that are in a state of flux and perpetual becoming.[39]

Based on the Brethren's cosmology, the structure of the world was analogous to that of the human body, and the workings of the universal soul in the cosmos were akin to the causal response of the active human bodily limbs to human volitions. The Brethren, moreover, held that the emanationist chain of being was mediated by the causal role assigned to the celestial spheres, whose motional vagaries get dramatically translated into blissful fortunes or tragic misfortunes. The sun and the moon, and Mars and the other planets, all have causal effects on our collective or individual everyday actions or eventful experiences. Furthermore, the preservation of the forms in matter, which sustains the existence of all composite entities, is warranted by the causal mediation of the celestial spheres that secure the beingness of beings. Given that all corporeal physical entities, namely the sublunar creatures and earthly beings, are composites of matter and form, the preservation of form in matter upholds their existence, for as long as the forms remain in matter, the corporeal physical entities will continue to exist.

The Brethren's ontological picturing of nature was articulated by way of a literal interpretation of the microcosm/macrocosm analogy. In the twenty-sixth tract of their *Rasa'il* compendium, they claimed that the human being is a microcosm. This assertion expressed their opinion concerning the constitutional beauty of the human being, which in their view rested on the harmony of formal proportions that hint at the metaphysical, moral, and political significance of aesthetic ordering principles.

---

39. This picture draws heavily on neoplatonic leitmotifs of emanation and causal ontological hierarchies, as well as on Platonist metaphysical binary models of same and other, being and becoming.

The human body was thus seen as a mere miniature reflection of the cosmos, whereby bodily limbs correlatively correspond with the parts that make up the whole of the universe. However, the patterns of similitude that animate this reading of the microcosm/macrocosm analogy not only highlighted corporeal configurations of resemblance, but also affirmed that the human soul emulates the motion of the world spirit. Based on a literal analogical reasoning, the Brethren even attempted to draw some forced structural similarities between the human limbs and the ecological and geographical constitution of the earth. This analogical equivalence was further reiterated in the thirty-fourth tract of their *Rasa'il*, wherein they attempted to show that the macrocosm is a macroanthropon, namely, that the cosmos was a colossal human being. Nonetheless, despite the shortcomings in their intellectual acumen, their popularized views give us a significant account of the adaptive assimilation of the classical sciences of nature by the medieval Arab urban coteries.

To further elucidate the manner by which an account of nature gets translated into an ontological inquest, we may briefly appeal to the consideration of the modalities of being in Avicenna's commanding thinking.[40] Based on logical and metaphysical grounds, the question of being is articulated in Avicenna's system from the standpoint of examining contingency, necessity, and impossibility. While necessary existence cannot but be, given that its negation entails an absurdity, impossibility cannot existentially be, given that its affirmation is a logical fallacy. As for contingents, they are brought into exis-

---

40. I have addressed Avicenna's ontology from the standpoint of Heidegger's critique of the history of metaphysics and the oblivion of the question of being in Nader El-Bizri, *The Phenomenological Quest Between Avicenna and Heidegger*, pp. 95–147, Binghamton, NY: Global Publications, 2000.

tence by way of a cause that is external to their essence. Consequently, a contingent does not sustain the reasons for its own existence within itself or due to its own essence.[41] A contingent cannot actualize its existential potentiality by itself, but is rather granted its existence by being the effect by necessity of an existent cause. In all of this, the distinction between the necessary and the contingent is informed by a pattern that is similar to what is attested to in Plato's *Timaeus*. Therein, a distinction is drawn between rest and motion, being and becoming, the intelligible archetype and the sensible copy, and the uncaused eternal form and the caused temporal physical entity.[42] However, when a contingent is brought into existence by way of an existential cause that is other than itself, it then becomes in its very actuality a necessary existent due to something other than itself. A contingent is hence a mere potentiality of existing due to itself and is an actual existent due to something other than itself. Causation thus articulates the existential sequence of dependency of all contingents insofar as in their actual existence they are necessary existents due to what is other than themselves. In this sense, all natural entities are contingent beings that have been brought into existence by way of existential causes. These beings have their existence distinct from their essence, and the nexus of causality that sustains their being leads back to the one and only necessary existent due to itself, whose essence is none other than its existence.[43] And it is by way of an undiminished

---

41. *Avicenna Latinus, Liber De Philosophia Prima Sive Scientia Divina I–IV*, p. 72, ed. S. Van Riet, introduction G. Verbeke, Leiden: E. J. Brill, 1977.

42. Plato, *Timaeus*, p. 28c, trans. R. G. Bury, Cambridge, MA: Harvard University Press, Loeb Classical Library, 1999.

43. I have addressed the ontological entailments of the distinction between essence and existence in Nader El-Bizri, "Avicenna and Essentialism," *The Review of Metaphysics*, 54:753–778, June 2001.

emanation that this one and only necessary existent due to itself brings about the existence of an effused universe, insofar as the concept of such a world is essentially contained in the idea of the necessary.

Like his neoplatonic predecessors, Avicenna's ontotheology may be characterized by naturalness.[44] Unlike the dialectical theologians, who might have influenced some aspects of his metaphysics of contingency, Avicenna did not sacrifice the notion of nature in view of defending an uncompromising creationist theory. Nonetheless, his ontology is not restricted to the domains of metaphysical or logical investigations, but rather is additionally determined by a bent on mysticism. His philosophical knowledge of nature is thus supplemented by an initium of spiritual gnosis and symbolism, which displaces nature by way of semiotic means in view of picturing it as the sphere of the systematic signs of divinity.[45]

## TECHNO-SCIENCE

The sophisticated theories of nature in the history of medieval Arabic sciences and philosophy found their practical maturation in the applied domains of technology.[46] This classical pragmatic bent on instrumentality pointed to an intrinsic tendency

---

44. Jean Joseph Houben, *Avicenna and Mysticism*, pp. 207, 217, 220, 221, Calcutta: Commemoration Publication, 1956.
45. Regarding the mystical bent in Avicennism, see Avicenna, *al-Isharat wa'l-tanbihat*, ed. Sulayman Dunia, Cairo: Dar al-ma'arif, 1960; Henri Corbin, *Avicenne et le Récit Visionnaire*, Tehran: Société des Monuments Nationaux de l'Iran, 1954.
46. For an abridged scholarly consideration of technology in the history of the Arabic/Islamic civilization, see Ahmad Y. al-Hasan, Donald R. Hill, *Sciences et Techniques en Islam*, translated into French by Hachem El-Husseini, Paris: UNESCO, 1991.

within the Arabic/Islamic medieval civilization to adopt an efficient course of action that is marked by expediency and convenience in handling the multifarious resources of nature, as well as venerating a metaphysical outlook that is driven by productivity and making.[47] The unfolding of the essence of technology would have further accentuated the contrast between nature and artifice, hence turning the position of the natural in culture increasingly ambivalent. For although God's creatures were to be heeded in Islam as symbolic of divine providence, their designated disposition to serve our human livelihood, compounded with technical advancement, may have gradually turned the blissful enjoyment of nature's bounties from a compassionate moderation in use to a mode of aggressive exploitation. The mytho-poetic graceful image of the world as symbolic of divine beatitude may have itself been compromised, or even partly evacuated, by the unfolding of an exacting instrumental techno-imagination that has been self-destined to enclose the beingness of beings. Having stated that, it must also be noted that this state of affairs was not restricted to the instrumental unfurling of the Arabic/Islamic medieval civilization as such, but was rather a universal phenomenon that is attributed to the very unfolding of the essence of technology. Initiated by the Greeks, forcefully elaborated by the Romans, and further developed by the Arabs and the Latins, it eventually led to the emergence of the techno-science of modernity.[48]

---

47. This state of affairs partly recalls what we encounter in Hegel's as well as in Heidegger's account of Roman religion as being energized by the spirit of an instrumental religiosity of convenience.

48. Heidegger attributes this phenomenon to the universal unfolding of the essence of technology, which in his view led to enframing beings as standing reserve.

Thinking about the relation between culture and nature, technological artifice and natural being, we may say that nature was
not always construed as necessarily imbued with goodness and
that on numerous occasions it naturally was the unfortunate
source of ills. This matter was, for instance, confirmed in the
classical Greco-Arabic art of healing, which oscillated between
a tendency to intrude on the patient, in view of prescribing artificial remedies, and a conservative romantic inclination to let
the human body take its natural course toward recovery. Due to
an all-encompassing worldview, the Greek Stoics and their Arab
followers had a faith in following the biological course of nature. Wisdom thus emanated from prudence with regard to the
naturopathic work of nature qua life and the observance of its
ways by reducing artificial intervention. Moreover, the eminent
Roman physician Claudius Galenus (A.D. 129–199), the inheri-
tor of the Greek medical edifice founded by Hippocrates (fifth
to fourth century B.C.), also celebrated the artistic tendency
(tekhnen) of nature, as it is noted in his treatise On the Natural Faculties (De Naturalibus Facultatibus).[49] And his tradition subsequently
found many exponents among the practitioners of medicine in
the Arabic/Islamic civilization, and it achieved its finest station
in Avicenna's Liber Canonis (Kitab al-Qanun fi'l-tibb).

Nature has evidently been the subject matter of copious doctrines in the history of ideas. The dedicated practitioners of science and the devout adherents to religion, each class in its own
persuasion, may have come to the realization that there was a
seeming order at work in the manner that nature regulated its
internal randomness and thusly mediated its inherent deviations
of chaos. From religious arguments of ontological design to
modern conceptions that are grounded in mathematics, nature

---

49. Galen, On the Natural Faculties, 6th printing, trans. A. J. Brock, Cambridge,
MA: Harvard University Press, Loeb Classical Library, 1979.

was broadly seen as governed by immanent principles. Pictured as a colossal scene of perpetual cycles of generation and corruption, nature was nonetheless construed by the Ancients (Greek, Arab, and Latin) as imbued by pointers and directives that led back to some form of divine providence, grace, or mercy. The classical conceptions of nature thus remained principally bound by ontotheological determinants until they were radically challenged by the surging modern scientific Cartesian and Newtonian paradigms.

In thinking about nature from an ontotheological monotheistic perspective, we attest to a contrastive metaphysical relation between creative nature and created nature.[50] For while the former was principally addressed from the standpoint of pure physics, the latter was primarily accounted for from the standpoint of theology. A similar pattern may also be attested to with the consideration of the notion of *humanitas*, namely whether it is to be attended to from the standpoint of ethics, politics, and psychology of the *homo natura*, or from the religious outlook of creation narratives or symbolic anthropocentric functions. Nevertheless, when we appeal to human nature at large, we acknowledge that it resists the essentialist encapsulation within rigid forms of definition, and breaks away from anticipated patterns of trait or predictable behavior. It is in this sense that civilization arises from the site where the instinctual natural impulses of humans get repressed by prescribed cultural supplements and derivative binding ethical principles. The radical conceptual distinction between nature and culture, which we attest to with the early modern techno-scientific diction, seems to be rather uncommon in previous intellectual all-encompassing archetypes. It is in this sense that the Latin *De Anima* literature (psychology),

---

50. Recalling thus the classic opposition: *natura naturens* versus *natura naturata*.

and its *Kitab al-nafs* Arabic correlate, continued to be integral to physics and natural philosophy.

With the exception of few remarkable figures in the history of Arabic sciences, like the polymath optician Alhazen (Ibn al-Haytham, d. 1039 C.E.), most Arab scholars kept the question of divinity well in view while engaged in their proto-scientific endeavors. While modern science pictured the universe as a book written in the language of mathematics, many Muslim theologians saw the world as a realm of divine ordinances. It is perhaps quite fair to say that the detachment of science from ontotheology on a universal level gained its full clarity with the maturation of the modern scientific revolution and its techno-logically motivated project. Perhaps this development may have reached its highest consummation with the presumed separation of techno-science from modern philosophy, a state of affairs grasped by some of our contemporaries as indicative of a Promethean era in thinking that is ominously marked by the closure of metaphysics and the end of philosophy.

from China

# *ZI RAN* (NATURE): A WORD THAT
# (RE)STRUCTURES THOUGHT AND LIFE

———

Chen Shao-Ming

Translated by
Li Lanfen

**THE WORD** 自然 (Zi Ran) occupies a unique position in the system of Chinese expressions. As a concept, it has been frequently employed in the history of Chinese ideas but has never been abstracted, as is the case with its English counterpart, *nature*, into an embracing category. In other words, one cannot concentrate on *Zi Ran* itself and follow its major semantic aspects unfolded in different historical situations with a view of mapping out the trajectory of the mutation of Chinese philosophical ideas. It is first and foremost an expression entrenched in everyday speech, content, so to speak, with its natural status, which, in turn, has made it so porous when it appears in theoretical discourses.

In everyday speaking and writing alike, *Zi Ran* can be used, without any morphological differentiation, as a verb, 自然而然, to follow the course of nature or the spontaneous inclination; as an adjective, describing attributes neither cultivated nor supernatural; and as a noun, which refers sometimes to the cosmic nature and sometimes to human instinct or desire. It can also stand for a lifestyle, an aesthetic taste or a social ideal. More often than not, the senses of this protean word overlap those of other linguistic signs. This results in a semantic cluster in the sense that some words may take the place of Zi Ran in speaking and writing but center around the notion Zi Ran conveys, while the semantic residue of each word as a substitute can be clearly or vaguely felt. This interaction renders the textual meaning of Zi Ran highly mobile and polysemous and, at the same time, necessitates some cross-reference to other words if one attempts a description of how Zi Ran as a key word keeps restructuring Chinese philosophical-political-social life. The key to the key word consists not so much in the intralinguistic autonomy of the word itself as in its extralinguistic contexts of situation. Only in the web or semantic cluster of "family resemblance" could one discern the roles Zi Ran plays in the process of Chinese verbal communications.

The following investigation falls into three distinct, though interrelated, parts: a historical survey of Zi Ran as a mobile idea, its operation as a shaping force in Chinese life, and its infiltration into modern political ideology. There will be no attempt at the establishment of a universal/homogeneous meaning intrinsic to the word Zi Ran. The focus is on how it works in different phases and fields.

## *ZI RAN* AS A MOBILE IDEA

The most important intellectual source of Zi Ran as a notion has been attributed to Taoism, a philosophical school active in the historical period from 400 to 200 B.C. Lao Zi and Zhuang Zi are the two representatives. One of the key propositions presented in the book *Dao De Jing* (or *Tao-te Ching* as sinologists used to say) written by Lao Zi is that Tao models itself after nature. This philosophical canon, however, does not offer an explicit definition in terms of Zi Ran. The word is only used with reference to all kinds of natural phenomena such as wind, rain, waters and seas, valleys, sounds, and colors. It suggests that one should follow the natural course or let nature take its own way. Diametrically opposed to human/social action, it also implies an exclusion of the personified divine. Such an admiration of Zi Ran (nature) in Lao Zi's context works, as a matter of fact, as an attempt to discredit the established value standards, which are based on a hierarchical arrangement of opposites: high versus low, hard versus soft, strong versus weak, etc. Taking water as an illustration, Lao Zi argues in his work that "the best (man) is like water. Water is good; it benefits all things and does not compete with them. It dwells in lowly places that all disdain. This is why it is so near to Tao." To follow the example set by water, Lao Zi points out: "Reversion is the action of Tao." Reversion of what? Civilization. Then, Zi Ran develops into an iconoclastic social ideal called Wu Wei: non-action. The term non-action does not mean inactivity but rather "taking no action that is contrary to nature."

For Lao Zi, non-action is not so much an end as a means: by virtue of Wu Wei, "there is nothing left undone." This is very different from Zhuang Zi's understanding, which regards non-action as an end in itself. Another difference between the two masters of Taoism is the substitution of Tien (heaven) for Zi Ran in Zhuang Zi's writings. In the first seven chapters of the book Zhuang Zi, identified by academic scholarship as Zhuang Zi's own work, one can hardly find the word Zi Ran. He turns to Tien (heaven) for expressing the idea of the cosmic nature, putting aside the idea of Providence or "home of God and the saints." The change in wording paves the way for a thematic shift from the nature/cultivation relationship to the heaven–human relationship, an abiding topic in the history of Chinese ideas. Back to the difference between Lao Zi and Zhuang Zi: the former lends the word Zi Ran to a social theory, while the latter, when talking about heaven as Zi Ran, emphasizes a personal attitude toward our lifeworld. In Chapter 2 and under the title of "The Equality of Things," Zhuang Zi tells stories about the harmony of the universe and forgetting about one's self, implying a possible world where there is no distinction between subject and object and between reality and unreality. To dislodge the self, according to Zhuang Zi, entails Wu Zhi (non-knowledge) and Wu Qing (non-passion). Non-knowledge precludes a utilitarian attitude of mind toward things, while non-passion holds at bay anxiety about one's own gain and loss. That is why they are also described as ultimate knowledge and the perfect passion capable of deconstructing the self-consciousness. It is clear that Zhuang Zi, in his work, does not advocate indifference but wishes to lead human emotion to the love of the whole universe and a disinterested aesthetic taste.

Zhuang Zi's arguments about heaven as nature separate him, as well as Taoism after him, from Confucianism, another school of thought that considers itself the champion of civilization by stressing the significance of social rites and enlightening music in terms of regulating human relationships. To the minds of Zhuang Zi and his followers, any slight accumulation of man-made civilization constitutes a serious encumbrance to the freedom of spirit, and therefore return to the "primitive" or natural condition is necessary and desirable. This hostility to human civilization and social institutions invites severe attack from Xun Zi, one of the greatest masters of Confucianism at that time, who ridicules Zhuang Zi's advice as "indulgent in Heaven and blind to man." Though his concept of heaven is close to the Taoistic interpretation and often translated into English as "nature," Xun Zi advocates in his works "dissolving biological instinct through social cultivation." The book of Zhuang Zi, when dealing with the problem of heaven as opposed to humans and of the self in relation to the external reality, has covered almost all the senses that reappear in later historical documents and that could be traced back, in one way or another, to the word Zi Ran. The only exception is that heaven or Zi Ran (nature) in Zhuang Zi excludes human instinct or desire, putting aside consequently the conflict within human nature.

Discussion about the heaven–human relationship continued in the Han Dynasty (206 B.C.–A.D. 220). Dong Zhong-shu, a Confucianism-styled scholar-politician, put forward a doctrine called "the correspondence of man and the numerical categories of heaven." It draws an analogy between various natural phenomena on the one hand and social institutions, moral laws, and even physiological structures on the other. Political control, in correspondence with heaven as nature, which is structured by the interrelationship of yin and yang, consists of legal punishment and moral government. The doctrine has gone so far as to match the number of bones in the human body with the number of days in the year. This reduction of social events and physiological knowledge to a mere copy of the supposed order of the universe stimulated at that time a retort from nonofficial intellectuals among whom Wang Chong was the most influential. Wang drew upon Taoism and came back to the term Zi Ran (nature) for the interpretation of Tien (Heaven). To deconstruct the teleology manifest in Dong Zhong-shu's doctrine, Wang tried to explain the mutability of natural phenomena as the operation of 气 (qi) or vital force, which was regarded as nonintentional and purposeless. (气, a key word in Chinese culture referring to a kind of material force, has various translations in Western sinology, such as breath, air, vapor, vital fluid, ether, and material force in English; *Wirkungskraft*, *Lebenskraft*, and *Oden* in German; and *air atmosphérique*, *soufflé du vent*, *vapeur*, *gaz*, *esprits vitaux*, etc. in French.) Of course, the antiteleological reinterpretation of Zi Ran also differs from the Taoistic recognition of the rational order of the cosmic nature.

The rise of the Metaphysical School during the Wei-Jin period (220–420) marks a theoretical syncretism of Taoism and Confucianism in terms of Zi Ran. Scholars started a hermeneutic project: to reconstruct the notion of Zi Ran by explicating historical classics including Lao Zi, Zhuang Zi, The Book of Change, and The Analects. In their works, Confucius appears like a naturalist, while Taoistic nonpassion, that is, the perfect passion, holds true for the cultivation of an ideal personality. As a human being, according to the Metaphysical School, the sage is not lacking in passion; he differs from others only in that he never falls prey to passion. On the other hand, disagreement existed among the Wei-Jin scholars concerning the relationship between Zi Ran (nature) and social institutions. Some argued that social institutions should conform to nature, while others held that social institutions themselves were natural. Nevertheless, both sides had two things in common: Taoistic in their metaphysics and Confucian in their social and political ideas. Opposed to this syncretism was a radical scholar named Ji Kang. Resistant to any cooperation with the political authorities, he regarded Confucianism, the state ideology, as a straitjacket used to suppress human nature. To his mind, the meaning of Zi Ran was not what Zhuang Zi understood as the exclusion of desire but "to follow desire and gain happiness." This position, one can see, is neither Confucian nor Taoistic. Since then Zi Ran has obtained another semantic dimension, opening up a view into the tension within human nature.

The predominance of neo-Confucianism (960–1644) over the Chinese theoretical activities largely reoriented the debate on the heaven–human relationship. With an attempt to rationalize the notion of heaven or nature, scholars created a new term 理 li (principle), similar to the Platonic "idea" or "form." The principle (li) of things conferred by heaven, they argued, constitutes man's original nature, while the mind is composed of a mixture of li and qi. In their contexts, qi stands for material force responsible for the production of existing things and for change. So, qi differs from the Western idea of matter, which is conceived of as inert and has to be shaped into substance by form. The li of all people is the same, but their qis vary from person to person and from situation to situation. When someone's qi is impure, he is foolish and degenerate. To retrieve the original nature, one must get rid of the impediment of this cloudy qi, especially desire. Obviously, this metaphysical explanation of the so-called original nature of man has excluded any possibility of the justification of human desires. Its impact upon Chinese thought has persisted for a long time. Disagreement among the Neo-Confucian School is exceptional. It was not until the late Ching (Manchu) Dynasty (from the late 1800s to the beginning of the 1900s) that scholars came out and protested against the murdering of human beings by means of the li. Among them, Kang You-wei was an outstanding figure. As a champion of political reform in the beginning of the twentieth century, Kang argued for the liberation of human desires from the suppression by the li, thus, turning the principle-over-desire structure upside down. Sympathetic to the newly introduced Western ideas including individualism and utilitarianism, Kang ushered in a new spiritual element for the modernization of Chinese culture.

## *ZI RAN*: A SHAPING FORCE IN THE LIFE WORLD

As a philosophical expression, Zi Ran proves to be a mobile notion. Its investigation reveals diachronic changes and results in a history of related ideas. In everyday life, however, it works as a shaping force: its semantic effects have cultivated a relatively stable system of beliefs and actions. It unfolds a picture of lifestyle rather than a philosophical conception. This lifestyle pivots on the Chinese perception of *Tien* (heaven) conceived of as the ultimate *Zi Ran* (nature).

In everyday conversation, heaven can stand for a kind of supernatural force capable of determining all human affairs by telling good from evil or right from wrong. This sort of power is referred to as "the intention of heaven." What is more, heaven's intention always manifests itself by means of natural phenomena. The term *Tien* (heaven) also signifies the order of the whole universe, a structuring force that makes life possible. Both the individual human beings and society as a whole are part of that order. Moreover, *heaven* is merely a synonym of *nature* in the sense of the cosmic nature or the natural environment as opposed to culture or human society. These three perceptions coexist, constituting the intertextuality of Chinese social life.

The first understanding is the most time-honored: its politicization started as early as the Zhou Dynasty (111–249 B.C.). Since then, the emperor had been referred to as "the son of heaven," while "grumbling at heaven's injustice" was regarded as ominous of social turbulence and political crises. In the *Book of Songs*, the first collection of ancient Chinese poetry, one can find that protest against the indifference or partiality on the part of heaven is a most popular theme. Owing to the influence of Dong Zhong-shu's doctrine, that is, the correspondence of humans and the numerical categories of heaven, people came to believe—and many still believe—that natural disasters function as a warning given by heaven, which finds the son's behavior incompatible with the way of heaven. The belief helps to account for the fact that political opponents in China often turn to the interpretation of natural disasters for their rebellious publicity. It also explains why the tribute to heaven, a national ceremony, was presided over always by the son of heaven, who would make some self-criticism and plead with heaven for mercy if there occurred serious natural disasters. The analogy between natural phenomena and social events is so well established that heaven worship still remains an important activity in the rural areas in South China. People even hold the view that lightning strikes a person because he/she has a bad conscience and gets the punishment from heaven. Nevertheless, this anthropomorphic tendency is more of pantheism than theism. The intention of heaven varies with the diversity of natural phenomena. In other words, the Chinese word *Tien* (heaven) cannot be related to God in the sense of Christianity. That is why Ricci, the Italian missionary, was condemned by the Vatican when he employed *Tien Zhu* (literally, the master of heaven) to translate the notion of God.

The second understanding of *Tien* (heaven) is closer to the Taoist attitude toward nature and proves to be shared by Confucianism. When talking about heaven as the order of the universe, Confucius said: "Does heaven speak? The four seasons pursue their courses and all things are continually being produced, but does heaven say anything?" Heaven is highly productive, and the mechanism of its productivity is described as the interaction of yin and yang. Lao Zi said: "Everything in the universe at once carries yin and embraces yang." Yin and yang have nothing to do with the concept of "substance," or attributes of that substance. Always going together, they stand for a function that makes possible the interdependence of two opposites. It explains the emergence of, as well as the interrelationship between, heaven and earth, summer and winter, hard and soft, right and left, male and female, emperor and subject, father and son, husband and wife, and so on, subsuming not only all natural phenomena but every state of affairs in society. Otherwise put, the yin–yang relation is understood as the specific working of the order of the universe. Then the anthropomorphic supernaturalism embodied in the notion of heaven merges into obscurity, and the intention of heaven no longer seems something beyond human comprehension. The more relevant problem is how to reach a unity of the order of human life and the order of the natural surroundings. A good example can be found in Chinese medicine according to which the structure of the human body epitomizes the order of the universe. It applies concepts like yin/yang and *Wu-shing* (five agents or elements: metal, wood, water, fire, and earth) to the interpretation of human physical life, very different physiologically and pathologically from medical science in its Western sense, though its therapeutic results are equally successful.

The above two understandings have one thing in common: both assume the interaction between heaven and humans, thus standing in contrast to the third one: heaven as something separate from culture or from the mind. Among the three, the second is the most influential with respect to everyday life. It proves to be a popular belief concerning people's relationship to their natural and cultural surroundings. Zhang Zai, a well-known neo-Confucianist, gave a brief account of the belief in his short treatise *Western Inscription*: "Heaven is my father and Earth is my mother. That which fills the universe I regard as my body and that which directs the universe I consider as my nature. All people are my brothers and sisters; all things in the universe are my companions; and the emperor is the eldest son of my parents (Heaven and Earth). . . . Respect the aged and take care of the young; help the poor and support the weak. This is the obligation of every member of the family/ universe. . . . Rejoice in Heaven and have no anxiety. This is filial piety at its purest." Obviously, the belief stresses a moral order entailed and justified by the order of nature. It informs a way of life, and at the same time provides an ontological basis for everyday moral practice.

The notion of the combination of heaven and humans becomes more practical and observable when emphasis shifts from the mental construction of the unity to the actual human relationships that are explained as connections made possible by nature. Liang Shu-ming, the famous modern Confucianist, once offered a summary of how it goes among the Chinese people:

We are born in relation to others and exist, until death, in that relation. Our life is the sum total of relationships, which give rise to the problem of ethics. Among all the relationships, family is primordial and therefore the most natural. Within the family, parents are primordial and then we have brothers and sisters. When grown up, we get married and have our own children, which is responsible for all kinds of blood connections. Once in society, we find ourselves in a more complex web of relationships. To learn something, we have a teacher–student relationship; to make money, we have an employer–employee relationship; to do politics, we have an emperor–subject or politician–voter relationship; to visit or help each other, we have a relationship between neighbors or friends. In one's whole life, countless relationships come into being. Each relationship constitutes an ethic. In that sense, ethics starts with family but does not confine itself within the family.

The above extrapolation from the natural tie (based on bloodline) to the social tie is regarded in the Chinese context as natural and referred to in a general way as heaven's relationship (*Tien Lun*). One of its functions in Chinese social life is the moral demand that one take others' aged as one's own and treat others' infants as one's own. And this is what is meant by "ethics starts with family but does not confine itself within the family." Here love is motivated by heaven's relationship or the analogy between nature (family connections) and culture (social connections) rather than the notion conveyed by "love your neighbor." Another example of the working analogy can be found in the Chinese system of appellation: *Shi Fu* (teacher-father) for one's teacher; *Tuzi Tusun* (student-son and student-grandson) for one's student and student's student; *Fumu Guan* (parent-official) for the state or local political authorities; Zi Min (children-people) for the masses as opposed to the parent-official. As for the relationship between neighbors or friends, people often use "brother" or "uncle" for identification. As a result, the whole society seems to be reduced to a state of family. In this native society, everyone is supposed to be familiar to everyone else. There is no room for strangers.

Xiao (filial piety) and Xing (an expression that integrates the meanings of sex, gender, and nature in the sense of human nature) are two important aspects regulated by the order of the universe. Xiao demands respect, deference, and attention from the young. It is also a reward for the nurturing one has received from the old. That explains in part why the Chinese, in addition to the sacrifice offered to heaven, devote time and energy to ancestor worship. To a certain extent, ancestry is more sacred and pertinent than heaven. Nevertheless, the highest form of filial piety consists in the perpetuating of the family through the reproduction of male successors in the patriarchal society. As a popular saying goes, "Among the three offenses against Xiao, failure to have a son is the most serious." Then, filial piety is functionally related to the end of Xing as sexuality.

Which is more natural and therefore more significant, sexual desire as such or human reproduction resulting from sexual activity as a means? There exists a lifestyle whose origin could be traced back to the Wei-Jin historical period (220–420 B.C.): local literati enjoy love affairs and feel proud of their unconventional, romantic behavior. To them, human reproduction is quite another thing. In contrast to that style of wild living, Confucianism-oriented minds tend to hold the topic of sex at bay. Two well-known novels might symbolize the polarization: The Golden Lotus and A Dream of Red Mansions. The first is an explicit and detailed description of various sexual activities, representing pornography within Chinese tradition, while the latter, though a love story, too, keeps sex at a safe distance and has been canonized as one of the greatest classics in the history of Chinese literature. Living within this tradition, one often plays a dual role: at once a serious reader in front of *A Dream of Red Mansions* and an anonymous voyeur of *The Golden Lotus*. Love is desirable, but sex, as far as the whole nation is concerned, still remains secondary to the continuity of the family as the most natural in life.

## *ZI RAN* AND POLITICAL IDEOLOGY

*State* and *country* are two distinct words in English but have to share one Chinese version *Guo Jia* (a compound word, literally country-family or state-family). On the one hand, the word *Guo* obscures the substantial difference between state and country, and on the other hand it joins itself to *Jia* (family) to make a unique concept. In Chinese, *Guo* and *Guo Jia* are identical. Interesting is the way of constructing this compound word. As the basic social unit, *Jia* (family) points to blood connections and belongs to nature, while *Guo* is the most unnatural social organization. Taken for granted, it helps to naturalize the ideological notion of "state" at the psycholinguistic level. But how did it happen in the beginning?

In remote antiquity, *Jia* was used to denote a male-centered community, much bigger than what the modern expression "family" could imply. Clan might be the right definition. A patriarchal *Jia* (family) in ancient times actually consisted of several clans genealogically related to one another. Later, a big *Jia* divided into several small ones, and each one possessed certain political/economic power in proportion to the position it occupied within that genealogy and its closeness to the ancestral origin. As the division continued, heads of smaller *Jia* (families) had to lead their people to new lands to be cultivated and walled. Those walled towns were important sources of material production and separated one *Jia*'s (family's) vested interests from another's. Here started a vague idea concerning political/economic power, which was visualized by the walled land but based on the bloodline. It was given the name *Guo Jia*, a linguistic condensation of the historical and "natural" evolution from *Jia* to *Guo*. The problem arising from that semantic syncretism is the indiscrimination of *Jia* (family) from *Guo*, and of *Guo* as "country" from *Guo* as "state." Fighting for or against one's *Guo Jia*, as an illocutionary act, could involve a holistic treatment of quite different ideas or things that ought to be considered separately. It encourages in Chinese life a unity of political loyalty and filial piety, a strategy adopted again and again by Chinese political leaders in the past two thousand years. One point is important and peculiar to Chinese culture: it is not external preachings but the syntax of the native language that in the first place helps to establish in the Chinese mind an image that blends family and country/state. Another trope follows naturally: the emperor or the supreme political leader as the father. It is this analogy between family and country/state or nature and culture that constitutes the theoretical foundation of the Confucianism-oriented sociology and political science in China. In everyday conversation, people often use *Gong Jia*—literally "public family"—to designate the state or the government and all its possessions. A recently composed song keeps echoing throughout China: "We Big Chinese, So Big a Family!"

The play on "public" leads to another issue. Since the beginning of the twentieth century, intellectuals have started to talk about *Gong De* and *Si De*, public morality and private morality. The latter concerns the relationships between parents and children, teachers and students, colleagues, neighbors, and so on, pointing to a world of acquaintances, while the former involves general relationships in a public community in which strangers are treated as equals. It is said and generally accepted that the Chinese pay more attention to private morality than to public morality. Making noise in a restaurant is a sign of lacking public morality. In spite of its inner contradiction, that is, "morality" presupposes "public" and cannot be "private," the real significance of *Gong De/Si De* opposition lies in the fact that the nature-determined blood connection is at the bottom of moral considerations. To put it in other words, if the ambiguity of *Guo Jia* (state/family) makes the naturalization of political power possible, then the priority of private morality over public morality paves the way for what is advocated in China as moral government. This is also a way of control that, in the Chinese context, depends on the measurement of specific interpersonal relationships, appeals more often than not to affectionate factors, and consequently renders the objective application of law in its modern sense more difficult. It also contributes to neglecting the necessary frontier that has to be drawn between the area of private life and that of public authority. As a result, intrusion upon privacy or illegitimate deprivation of an individual's freedom occurs in the name of benefiting the public or *Guo Jia*. On the other hand, every individual has a chance of appropriating things belonging to the public family and yet can sleep with a calm conscience. Of course, the more public power one possesses, the more private interests one can obtain.

This private/public paradox reached its climax in the operation of the people's commune. As a political/economic organization in China's rural area, the people's commune combined several villages into one community. It aimed, first of all, to substitute for the traditional family/clan-based power structure and reduce the complicated human relationships to a simplified hierarchical division of social classes. Unfortunately, with the private morality prevailing over public morality, class consciousness proved to be favoritism. At the economic level, the people's commune put an end to the private ownership of the means of production and let the peasants depend on the state/family (*Guo Jia*) for a living. It was a big "family" and everyone wished to get something out of it. Again, the more power one held, the more one got.

The structuring force of *Guo Jia* (state/family) or *Si De* (private morality) facilitates a more or less traditional strategy of making political ideas something natural. Behind the strategy is the collective assumption as regards the relation of heaven to humans. Progress in scientific studies of both natural phenomena and cultural artifacts has shown, however, that the combination of heaven and humans is more an attitude of mind than a matter of fact in the actual world. The attempt at the naturalization of political ideas has to turn to another interpretation of *Zi Ran* (nature) for legitimacy: material as opposed to mind.

Doctrines in the history of Chinese ideas are favorably defined as "simple materialism" if they foreground a purely material and nondivine dimension. Its function in terms of constructing contemporary ideology is threefold: it helps to stir up a revolution for a new social system that is presumably capable of satisfying the basic material needs the old regime failed to; it justifies the efforts made for the modernization of industry and agriculture and promotes a profit-based work ethic; and, attached to the framework of the theory of evolution, it encourages the idea of social progress with communism as the final end. Nature here is separated from the mind and regarded as the object of subjugation with a view to achieving material prosperity. But materialism in the Marxist context does not merely mean the physical world or the cosmic nature. In the form of historical materialism, it also refers to social, especially economic, existence as a material force, thus involving many nonphysical things. The established intersubjectivity is also material in nature. Thanks to that signification, the status quo finds its justification through a biased explanation of the famous proposition of "being determines thinking."

Another problem with the materialist understanding of Zi Ran (nature) comes from the reinterpretation of communism in the Chinese cultural context. As a social ideal, communism tends to be reduced to a moral principle: altruism. Then this moral principle is associated, in one way or another, through all kinds of propaganda, with the conceptions of "the public," "the Party," "the people," "the political authorities," and so on. All this stands as the opposite to instinct, desire, material interests, and everything else that the term nature strives at. To avoid the contradiction, the ruling ideology has to turn for help to the dichotomy of body and soul, matter and mind, or material and spiritual. It is the same mode of cognition that, in the first place, makes Zi Ran as something independent of the mind possible. It goes both ways. When it is difficult to meet people's material needs, moral preachings about the priority of spiritual life, together with its implication about political obedience and conformity, might work. It used to be described as the difference between the noble idea of communist spirit and the decadent bourgeois way of living. Nowadays, with success in material reconstruction, we find another expression or jargon for the self-reference of the ruling ideology: spiritual civilization. The cooperation of two civilizations, material and spiritual, advocated by the establishment, reflects its attempt to deal with the constant tension between spontaneous desire and ideological control or between nature and culture in the specific Chinese context. In the final analysis, political ideology in China cannot help but make full use of, and get caught in, the contradictory but interrelated comprehensions of Zi Ran. Whether it comes up in the form of Tien (heaven) or manifests itself through an intermediary like Guo Jia, the three senses of Zi Ran could be located, in one way or another, in any official attempt at the naturalization of political ideology.

from Europe

# FABLES OF NATURE

———

Pierre Zaoui

Translated by
Robert Bononno

*We other Europeans, admirers of Nature . . .*
—Friedrich Nietzsche, Human, All Too Human


**CONCERNING NATURE, IT WOULD** be difficult to find a shared European sensibility or shared set of concepts, much less a common morality or politics, only a swarm of images, notions, and political and moral precepts that are as vague as they are contradictory. More than a century ago, Nietzsche claimed that our age was no more than a "multicolored painting of all that has ever been believed." In this slapdash image nature still plays a key role. A vast, imprecise kaleidoscope, denigrated or praised, it allows us to justify and condemn by turns, enveloping everything within itself or rejecting everything. Although we never stop talking about nature, we do so in a circular manner. In fact, we no longer know what it is.

Although we are unable to define it, or even present a linear history of its dominant representations, which tend to merge with one another over time, we can, nevertheless, still ask our-selves why nature is, and has always been, an idea and a subject of importance, simultaneously necessary and obscure, demanded by reason or sensibility though produced by the imagination (fable, model, or anti-model). Although we don't know what it is, and although each of its specific representations seems to fall within the framework of tales and legends, we can legitimately question this sempiternal need to mythologize it as something whole and permanent. The nature of things or human nature, order or disorder, system or chaos, necessity or accident, we always experience the need to conceive of a nature that supports, stimulates, or threatens human reason.

On first examination we can identify three major contempo-rary fables about nature, or rather, three types of explanation for this fictional need. Initially, we can state that nature in itself does not exist. Every fact said to be natural is the result of a con-struction or an interpretation; in truth there are only artifacts, only culture. Nature's meaning is relative to a given culture. And it could be said to express that culture's need to create for itself a legendary other, which will serve as a regulatory principle (for its science), a classificatory principle (for its morality and poli-tics), and an aesthetic principle (for its art). This is the approach taken by the majority of the social sciences based on eighteenth-century empiricism, and most likely by any ecology in the pri-mary sense of the term (the study of ecosystems). Hume said that "the science of human nature is the only social science." We don't know what nature is, but we know what our environ-ment is, our ecosystem, our natural body, as today's environ-mental scientists might say. Yet such an approach merely sidesteps the problem. If there is no nature, only a secondary nature, that is, a human nature or human environment, described by an anthropology or an ecology (unifying geology and biol-ogy), what then is the nature of this human or environmental nature? In doing so we risk simply transferring to humans or the earth the legends we ordinarily attribute to the world.

In response to this danger, one could say that if we no longer know what nature is, it's because we have forgotten its original meaning, its true initial sense not relative to a culture or a discipline, but to an a priori understanding of the way in which the idea of nature originally assumed meaning for a consciousness or for a creature of flesh and blood. Setting aside empirical data, which is assumed to preexist and to be known, and positive science (geometry, physics, anthropology), what is it that originally gives meaning to things, to space, to time, and to existence in general? Why do we perceive nature as nature, as something that exists? Since phenomenology has taken the problem seriously, we may well ask what its approach has been. If nature is a need both speculative and practical, it is legitimate to investigate it: Where does it come from? On what basis does it assume meaning? From consciousness, our body of flesh and blood, or from our place of birth? However, such an approach may do more to complicate the problem than to solve it. On the one hand, it grants everything to nature, for modern techno-science in its enthusiasm for control, rather than welcoming the truth of phenomena, overlooks and ridicules nature continuously. On the other hand, it drains it of life. If everything depends on providing a meaning to or questioning nature, then the nature conceived of as a given exteriority (nontranscendent) absolutely does not exist. At bottom, in and through its attachment to things themselves, phenomenology incorporates a radical antinaturalism that denies any primal reality to physical, biological, or anthropological facts in the name of hyperrationalism, indeed, for some today, even in the name of religion.

Finally (and this is the position I would like to defend), we recognize the ineluctably problematic character of the idea of nature by maintaining that, if it's a fable, it is nonetheless a fable we need to live and to conceive of other possible worlds. The need to mythologize would then no longer be relative to a particular culture, it would relate to the universal possibility of a critical attitude toward an actual society or culture: criticizing an institution or representation requires first that we always imaginatively proffer a plan of nature we assume to be given for everyone, and valid for all human and nonhuman activities. Any nondogmatic critical approach assumes that we imaginatively supply ourselves with an unofficial nature that provides criteria with which and on behalf of which criticism becomes possible. For without reference to an objective nature, whatever it may be (nature of the world or the nature of mankind), any criticism of the established order becomes impossible since the latter sweeps away all reality along with it: everything is arbitrary, therefore anything is permitted. Yet only the affirmation of its ineluctably imaginary character prevents critical action or speech from degenerating into a religion of authority and neoconservatism. In examining the history of the idea of nature, we find that from Empedocles to political ecology, including along the way Lucretius, Giordano Bruno, Galileo, Spinoza, the French and Anglo-Scottish Enlightenments, Nietzsche, Marx, and Deleuze, it is always with reference to a return to a lost continuity between humans and nature that great critical ideas have been elaborated. And this is true of philosophy as well as politics, science as well as art, the idea of nature designating neither a physical given nor its foundation, in other words, neither the real as it can be perceived nor an ideal, or utopia, but the inextricable and multiple conjunction of the two.

From this point of view there is no opposition between nature and artifice, or religion and science, or classic rationalism and renaissance or romantic illuminism, since nature becomes the exact point at which the various dimensions of any critical position meet and combine. Nature would no longer be second-ary or radically primary, but always constructed as a first fabulous reality. It would be a kind of true fiction. Of course, such naturalism, too vitalist for the positive sciences, too realist and artificial for phenomenology, could not be associated with a historically determined way of thinking. The fable of a nature that is recognized as such while remaining natural, that is necessary and directly engaged with immediate reality, can be found in positions that are no doubt too unique to reveal any consistent line of thought. But there is little doubt that all of these critical movements derived from it, at least before theology reduced it to a pure object of belief or positivism associated it with a handful of confirmed but lifeless facts.

Such contrasts are not new. As far back as the Greeks, nature appeared this way—simultaneously as a political fable, a fable of the origin of things, and a critical fable of itself, that is, critical of its reification as an intangible principle of order. In many ways common sense demands as much: If there is a nature, the very idea of a "history of nature" is a contradiction in terms.

Thinking about nature has always been circular, critically, phenomenologically, and naturalistically. No doubt there is a history of concepts of nature or the world, of a weltanschauung, but there may not be a history of the profound idea of nature, whose essence would lie precisely in its insuperable, and thus ahistorical, ambiguity. This is what remains to be proven.

## THE LAYERED AMBIGUITY OF THE GREEKS

In general we speak of nature among the Greeks, from the earliest pre-Socratic physicists to the Hellenistic philosophies (stoicism, epicureanism, skepticism), either to remind ourselves of the progress made since those poetic and prescientific dark ages, or on the contrary to refer to a healthy return to a primal but forgotten nature. It is uncertain, however, that the Greeks' idea of nature was much clearer than our own.

This is certainly true of the pre-Socratic philosophers, who can be read as critics of the common idea of nature as well as its defenders. Whatever differences they may have had, what seems to unite Heraclitus and Democritus, Empedocles and Parmenides, is the idea that humans have lost the meaning of nature, have made it into a simple passive image, or have lost interest in it entirely. "Nature loves to hide itself," wrote Heraclitus (fragment 123). And Empedocles went further when he stated, "Nature is not what our senses tell us, but is not something beyond the senses." And if the first philosophers were primarily concerned with defining nature, it's because for them it was a problem before being a concept or transparent intuition—and a problem that was simultaneously metaphysical (what is being?), scientific (how does the world function? what is history?) and politico-religious (how can we live well in nature?). From this point of view, it was less the images they used that were important—Thales spoke of water, Heraclitus of fire, Empedocles of fire (principle of disunion, of hate), then water (principle of union and mixing, of love)—than the question of which image was best. Cosmogonic myths, "naturalist" descriptions, speculative meditation, political injunction, sometimes pious, sometimes apparently impious, follow one another in their fragments, even though it is not really possible to say what they mean exactly by *phusis*, or "nature."

A simple aphorism, Delphic before it was Socratic, does a good job of summarizing this radical ambiguity: "Know thyself." On the one hand, it signifies that it is within you that you will find the true meaning of things, the world, and your life. From this viewpoint early Greek naturalism appears to be entirely focused on humankind. Nature is first of all a problem of morality and religion; it is inside before being outside. Yet it also means find your place in the universe, know who you are through the place you occupy. It is a naturalism without humans, diametrically opposed to our modern, individualistic, and psychological humanism. We find the same fundamental ambiguity, although in more systematic fashion, in Aristotle. Initially, nature is *phusis*, that is, growth, generation, an interior and vital temporality, the spontaneous movement of life toward its form or its place; it is neither matter nor accident, neither form nor necessity, but another, obscure power that informs matter, actualizes power, probabilizes chance, orders the disparate. This is an essential point for biology. Nature is the principle of life and the organization of the living. Correlatively, therefore, nature is *telos*, that toward which all things tend. This is essential for physics. The natural world is sustained by a network of predetermined finalities that make it legible and relatively ordered—nature does nothing in vain. However, this also has consequences for morality and politics. There is a law of nature, or natural law, that is the source and legitimizing principle for every moral norm and every positive law, enabling us to discriminate between the just (according to nature, *kata phusin*) and the unjust (against nature, *para phusin*), and establish the excellence or virtue of all things.

Yet generation sometimes entails corruption, and if nature is an end, this means that people, like all things, are not "natural" (virtuous, just, excellent) "by nature." In other words, nature, like being, is never an unequivocal principle, but immediately implies its opposite. It can thus serve to magnify life (within us— our dispositions—or without us—things, places, moments) or demean it (within us—"bad character"—or without us— corruption); to provide a rational principle for understanding the world or create an obstacle to the only efficient causality of the moderns; to outline an initial phenomenology of things and space or ignore them in the name of common sense; to split it-self off from religion or return to it (the question of God as prime mover concludes Aristotle's *Physics*).

Second, nature is *cosmos*, a closed and ordered world consist-ing of a system of fixed and hierarchically arranged places: (1) the sphere of changeless things that encloses the world and where God, the "prime mover," dwells; (2) the moving planets, whose movement is perfect (circular); and (3) the world beneath the moon, the place of contingency and imperfect movements. Apparently, it appears as a unified whole in which each thing has its place (or results from violent movement, that is, against nature). But in truth there are two worlds: the extralunar world, the world of necessity and perfection, and the sublunar world, the world of contingency and corruption (thinking that one lives at the center of the world is not a sinecure or sign of human pride as Freud incorrectly believed). Here, too, unity is eaten away by a more profound duality, order by a principle of disor-der, clarity by a more opaque mystery.

Faced with this profound and hardly satisfying ambiguity, Lucretius, a late poet and philosopher, writing in Latin rather than Greek, attempted to transmute this difficulty into a multi-plicity of songs explicitly affirming nature as a poetic, but nec-essary, fable, thereby freeing himself from fear of the gods and the religions of salvation (in another world); that is, he main-tained a critical attitude toward the established order under cover of an assumed natural order. The product of chance and encoun-ter, both matter and growth, a "shower of atoms" (the physi-calist model) and "vital fluid" (biological model), nature becomes not a dualistic principle of unsuspected ambiguity, but a poetic plan unifying all the heterogeneous dimensions of thought and action, to which no one can claim to hold the se-cret key—not the scholar, the politician, or the priest. Nature is the common good of all, which everyone can mythologize for

their own personal use. The *rerum natura*, or nature of things, signifies anything but a unique anthropocentric, or, on the contrary, dehumanized model. It is a principle of continuity and
universal communication between humans and nature, a song
that is inseparably ethical, political, scientific, and poetic.

## MIDDLE AGES AND RENAISSANCE:
## THE REDISCOVERY OR INVENTION
## OF NATURE?

The Lucretian song could very well be the swan song of classical naturalism, since for nearly fifteen centuries, until the Renaissance, the cult and study of nature, although not ready to
disappear, seemed about to fade into the background, shoved
aside by the primacy of revelation and theology. At first medieval Christianity appeared to harbor a radical a-cosmic and
antinaturalist stance. Created by God, nature, both inside and
outside humans, no longer contained the immanent principle
of its comprehension. It could only be apprehended in itself and
for itself, its meaning was only derivative. Worse, sullied and
obscured by original sin, it appeared more a source of decep-
tion than of transparency, of vanity than glory (*contemptus mundi*:
contempt for the world as a form of virtue), of temptation than
wisdom. And it assumed different forms, all of which reflected
its secondary and heteronymous status.

The monastic orders called it a "desert," in opposition to the
world, the "region of dissemblance." Being in nature meant
"going to the desert," a place from which God was absent, with
no sensible manifestation in the heart of humans—absence and
exile. Nature became the nonplace where one could find oneself by separating from the world. It then came to be an *empire*,
the realm of God, and humans an empire within that empire,

imperium in imperio, as reflected in the sweeping analogy between microcosm and macrocosm that was common until the Renaissance. There are two natures, two worlds, that of things and that of people, which reflect one another analogically according to a principle of similarity that is outside them. Here as well nature is anything but an object of contemplation and autonomous science. It is the mark, the sign of something else, of a supernature that must be discovered outside itself. This resulted in the two dominant metaphors of nature as theater, the abstract stage on which salvation and damnation were played out regardless of the set design, or as a book to be deciphered in the hope of discovering the keys to another world. In both cases it did not exist for itself, it was not object but mediation toward its opposite: "Therefore prescribe charity from the world and not with the world, nor toward the world," wrote Hugues de Saint-Victor at the beginning of the twelfth century. Medieval iconography itself has no background and is abstract. As with theology, nature is only a theater without even the illusion of naturalism, or a book—the symbolism of the ignorant.

Yet all of this can change. Nature as a collection of creatures is no longer a lost Eden, but neither is it a "vale of tears," since it has been created by God. Although a desert, it is still "our land," "the garden" offered to the sons of men, or the "temple" where the expected encounter with God will take place, as Saint Bernard wrote in his commentary to the Song of Songs. Theology and mysticism are filled with hymns to nature, God's offering to mankind: "O daughter of God, genetrix of all things, world's connection, stable knot, gem in the earth," sings Alain de Lille. Saint Francis of Assisi and Bonaventura established the foundations of a Christian naturalism, where every thing, every bird, every insect is no longer a simple sign but seems to be the bearer of an element of divinity. Saint Thomas's philosophy recaptures the Aristotelian idea of a nature that is the source of norms and splendors. Similarly, human nature is dualistic: although it has lost its resemblance to God, it has, nonetheless, retained the image—a deceptive image—and thus merits praise as well as blame, love as well as contempt.

From this point of view we cannot rely too much on the renascent ideology that claims to rediscover nature and open it up toward infinity after ten centuries of blindness. It is true that iconography was radically transformed with the invention of perspective and the presence of nature in the background. Landscapes became an object of contemplation in themselves—one could speak of the "invention of landscape" in reference to Petrarch's *Ascension of Mont Ventoux*—and with Nicolas de Cues and Bruno, nature becomes infinite, with Galileo and Torricelli, the source of experiment. But it would also be easy to point out its continuity with medieval ambiguity. The simultaneous invention of perspective and landscape can also be seen as a process of the radical artificialization of nature: invention is not discovery. Moreover, the rediscovery of naturalism is inseparable from the rediscovery of humanism, which, by raising humans, lowered nature. The medieval metaphors of nature as a book or as a theater experienced an extraordinary renewal of interest at the time. They are omnipresent in Erasmus (nature is the theater of man's folly), in Galileo (nature is *written* in mathematical language), in Montaigne (where the whole social world is theatrical artifice). More than ever, what is important is the text, the ancient writings. This new naturalism is as much a rebirth of the observation of nature as its erudite abstraction, Platonist, even magical. And it was a period when books of magic and thaumaturgy flourished. The conventional description of the Renaissance as naturalist and humanist reflects less a celebration of a rediscovered unity than the acknowledgment of the renewal of an ancient contradiction. Here as well, there is no epistemic break or clear and unequivocal aesthetic. The earliest indications of the mathematization, experimentation, and technologization of nature are associated with its disenchantment as well as its re-enchantment. And they were enacted as much against religion (Bruno was burned, Galileo condemned) as for it (Cusain's infinite naturalism, Montaigne's skepticism in the service of the faith).

Nature thus remains the source of the most contradictory claims. Both unitary and dual, hostile and enriching, infinite but always closed ("worlds" became infinite, not space), observable and mysterious, continuously rediscovered or reinvented (thus lost as nature), the history of its representation continues to dissimulate rather than reveal the true revolution under way—in mathematics, experimentation, and technology, in other words, through artifice. Does this imply that the real transition didn't fully come to light until the age of classicism?


## MECHANISM AND VITALISM FROM THE CLASSICAL AGE TO THE ENLIGHTENMENT

With the onset of classicism, old and new "cosmic attitudes toward nature," as Cassirer called them, disappeared, only to be replaced by a new, entirely material nature that was morally and religiously neutral, and rationally transparent. However, there may have been too much insistence on the upheavals that, during the seventeenth and eighteenth centuries, led to the "disenchantment with the world," described by Max Weber. Nature became a material extent or simple mechanism entirely accessible to scientific and technical rationalism since it had been stripped of its occult qualities and "souls" (the ancient principles of movement), its analogical and supernatural similarities, its animals and sorcerers, its enclosed places and mysteries. It would no longer be a source of praise or blame, but simply of observation and mastery. This reading was not related to the idea of nature as such but to the birth of an entirely different concept, that of the manipulable environment, conceived as an intermediate realm between the here and now and the great whole. Until that point we could not really speak of an environment. There were enclosed spaces (cities, the sublunary world or *topoi* of common knowledge) that came into direct conflict with an unknown exterior (the dwelling place of the gods and the wild animals). Like the sentiment of nature, this idea seemed to crystallize the problematization of the link that connects this enclosed interiority to an unknown exterior. In the classical age there arose an intermediary environment that, although it did not resolve the problem of the link, was able to thrust it aside. In any event, this is the meaning of the word *like* in the famous Cartesian slogan enjoining us to "become like a master and possessor of nature," "like" because real nature belongs to God, who is its only master, whereas we are masters only of a "second" nature, *indeterminately close* rather than infinite, and created each instant according to plans that will forever remain unknown to us. In other words modern science and technology are only able to realize the ancient fantasy—Jewish and Greek—of man's domination of nature, but obscure it behind the future notion of the environment.

During the classical age, the apparent techno-scientific reduction of an ancient dualistic nature, radically ambiguous, luminous and hidden, to an unequivocal, homogeneous, and controllable matter, corresponds less to a change in the paradigm of nature than to the simple, although premature, emergence of a new one, that of the environment. In other words the concept of nature did not fundamentally change meaning, it simply faded into the background, behind the environment, understood as the "milieu of human life." And this environment was equally foreign to a radically exteriorized and cosmic nature as well as to a radically interior nature, the intimate nature of humans. From this point of view today's anthropocentric environmentalism, which justifies its ecological focus by the desire to preserve the conditions for the survival of the human species, is much more the distant heir of Descartes, Hobbes, and La Mettrie than of their detractors. This is because we have become like masters and possessors of the planetary environment for which we are responsible; it is because nature is no longer thought of as nature (origin or totality) but as a single paradigm of the environment that yesterday's claim to transform it and today's desire to preserve it have the same meaning. I want to put forth four arguments in support of this hypothesis.

First, we have insisted strongly on the transition, between the Renaissance and the Enlightenment, from a closed world to an infinite universe (Cassirer, Koyré). If this is true for physics and astronomy, this transition and its influence on attitudes toward nature should be relativized twice. Initially in terms of another revolution, one that was slow to begin but picked up speed with time—the discovery of the New World and its subsequent colonization. Nature no longer appeared as infinite and pure exteriority, but as pure finite interiority without an exterior. Two centuries later, the British empire would be praised as one on which the sun never set. The change must also be relativized by the discovery of the infinitely small. Shortly after the first telescopes, the first microscopes were invented, a stunning development that introduced a totally unknown nature, filled with new mysteries but again cut in two (Pascal would describe man as a "bridge between two infinities").

Second, whether through a concern for historical priority or the effect of the signifier, we are wrong to reduce the modern vision of nature to new physical concepts alone. Modern nature belongs not only to Newton but to Buffon as well, an organic nature, vitalist and teleological. In support of this we have the far-reaching "argument of vital forces," where the greatest thinkers of the seventeenth century addressed the problem of force:

What then is the notion of natural force on which modern science and politics was built? In other words, the science of nature remains dualistic—one part focused on space, another on life—and obeys two resolutely antagonistic epistemological models. Moreover, there is some doubt that we will ever manage, even today, to reduce the second to the first. In all cases, unless we take into account this dualistic conception of nature, we can never understand the resurgence, in the eighteenth century, of a robust interest in naturalism that fell halfway between physics and biology (Diderot seems to have been unable to decide between the two models), or physics and anthropology (Hume could only speak of the "obscure" principles of nature, such as habit and sympathy, irreducible to its "clear" principles of experience and egoism), or between science in general and religious illumination (found in the Bishop Berkeley of the Siris, or in the appeal to a "sentiment of nature" characteristic of German Sturm und Drang that ushered in the philosophies of nature among the romantics).

Third, and in a more specifically political vein, we are wrong to describe modernity as the final abandonment of a nature that is a source of norms and, therefore, as the secularization (or historicization) of politics and the end of its subordination to morality (Leo Strauss). True, with Machiavelli and Hobbes natural law no longer seems to signify anything other than force, amenable to a physics of forces rather than a politics based on justice. But this reduction did not last long, and it was against the background of the ancient and medieval "law of nature" that a new, ideal conception of modern natural law was built, one that expressed the fundamental and inalienable liberties of humankind in general. In other words, we should not overlook Rousseau, Kant, and the *Declaration of the Rights of Man and of the Citizen*. With the advent of the modern age, politics does not abandon the idea of nature, but treats it as a battleground, intermingling the simplistic oppositions between ancients and moderns, progressives and conservatives, liberals and royalists.

Fourth and last, it seems especially difficult to identify a single noncontradictory attitude toward nature in the classical age and the Enlightenment. Although its extension toward infinity fed the optimism and renewed thirst for knowledge found in Descartes, Leibniz, and Newton, this renascent sense of optimism also served as a source of silence and anxiety in Pascal. Somewhat later, although it is identified with the sublime in Kant (mountains, hurricanes, storms), Hegel associates nature with a radical impoverishment and replaces it with art, or even history, as the guarantors of an infinite totality of meaning. While it is experienced as the voice of good and morality in Rousseau, it seems to have been no more than an experience of the monstrous and the sublime in evil for Burke, if not the source for legitimizing such evil (Sade). Thus, it is not saying much to claim that the beginnings of our "modernity" turned out to be as powerless to produce a unified sentiment of nature as they were an unequivocal epistemological model. Confronted with the strident revolution of technology, the eternal problem of the link between humans and nature, institution and instinct, construct and given, remains unheard.

## THREE CONTEMPORARY FABLES OF NATURE

I want to cut short the historical detour since it is far from obvious that the nineteenth and twentieth centuries can add anything more to my argument. Once stated, the model of scientific determinism soon begins to vacillate, initially with the second law of thermodynamics, entropy, then with quantum physics, the irreversibility and uncertainty of nature partially reasserting their rights without dissolving the general principle of determinism, that is, the intelligible necessity of natural (that is, sensible) phenomena. Similarly, in aesthetics, dandyism, then abstraction do not so much succeed a renewed naturalism as they add to it. In a sense, it is in the name of nature that we must acknowledge Wilde's dictum that "nature imitates art." Proust described art in terms of "optical instruments," thus providing a naturalistic interpretation of this imitation. Similarly, it is in the name of a more profound nature that naturalism would be denounced as academicism, impressionism as bourgeois art, and abstraction announced as the next big thing: Picabia, Dubuffet, and Yves Klein all thought they were primarily painters of matter. In politics even Marx seems to have been ensnared by the same eternal ambiguities, on the one hand, invoking Epicurus and Lucretius and calling for a new "continuity of man and nature," and on the other hand, appearing to give himself fully to a blind faith in technological progress and industrialization, rejecting any form of naturalist nostalgia. The nineteenth and twentieth centuries, like history in general, have thus turned out to be powerless to identify the divisions or obvious trends in our representations of and attitudes toward nature. And we continue to misuse language when speaking of "modernity" with respect to nature or, worse yet, "postmodernity." Nature has always been and remains a miscellany of fable and legend, whose history it is less critical to follow than its geography, or an admiring but skeptical recension.

There are three ways to consider this nature of fable: we can denounce it, regret it, or affirm it. At this level (and this level only), there are no more ambiguities but only clear oppositions that force us to make distinctions. Therefore, I want to discuss some of these options since they may indicate much deeper splits in contemporary European awareness, crisscrossing as they do a variety of disciplines: scientific, intellectual, artistic, and political.

## POSITIVIST ANTINATURALISM

We could call positivist antinaturalism the tendency to deny the existence of any true idea of nature, seeing it at best as no more than a naive, prescientific fable, at worst as an arbitrary, if not ideological, principle used to justify certain unfounded postulates or political values. In fact, this is what all positivist systems have in common, from August Comte and the human sciences to Viennese and English logical positivism: we know only facts or states of affairs, and the world is reduced to a legal or logical juxtaposition of those facts. We have no idea of nature as such, or of life, or of a whole that would be more than the sum of its parts—metaphysical terms devoid of meaning for positivists. If nature doesn't exist, therefore, if there exists only a logical or cultural world of facts, effectively, there is no more ambiguity. Naturalist fables are no more than "fly catchers"— mystical tales, Wittgenstein called them—and we must be satisfied with tautological statements. Naturalist fables are facts that must be reduced to factual utterances according to a principle of hermeneutic charity, or explained as cultural or historical facts (relativism and historicism are conflated here). In both cases, the idea of nature no longer establishes any norm or legitimacy; it is only a relic, a belated thought. That is what makes such thought important for progressives: the abolition of slavery, the affirmation of equality among citizens, feminism, the defense of homosexuality, seem to have been constituted, at least in Europe, on the basis of a rejection of the idea of nature. There are no slaves "by nature," no inequality or feminine nature, no "sins against nature," and so on.

What is important is to note the astonishing convergence of thought around this point (and this point only), between the empiricist or pragmatic epistemology of the hard sciences, the social sciences, the arts, and a progressive political stance. All of them agree enough to state that the difference between the fact (a natural given) and the artifact is not a priori but a posteriori (can it be verified?, does it work?). In other words, the idea of nature assumes meaning only within a determinate cultural or logical context. This is certainly true of science, where supposedly natural facts completely change their appearance and meaning according to the field of specialization involved, or according to the specific protocols of a given experiment: the natural bodies of the biologist are not the natural bodies of the physicist. Within physics, macrophysical bodies have nothing in common with quantum bodies. The same situation can be found in the social sciences. In geography, for example, Gaston Roupnel has shown to what extent the back-to-nature movement in France is always a return to the vestiges of an older culture: there is no tree, no field, no path that is not man's work. In anthropology Lévi-Strauss insisted on the fact that every culture affirms itself only by rejecting all the others in the realm of nature: nature is still a culture, just not one's own. Ulrich Beck, a sociologist, has continued to explain how our industrial societies have produced a "societization of nature," which prevents us from conceiving of a nature that is external to our processes of techno-scientific investigation.

The same is true for the positivist or symbolic history of art (Panofsky, Schapiro), which, ever since the Renaissance, has deconstructed every new naturalism, including those of the technical arts (photography and cinema). During the Renaissance, nature was only a geometrized ideal, just as Impressionist nature remains the sign of a gentrified nature. It was the response to the call for a return to the materiality of painting and sound that ushered in the transition to abstraction in the twentieth century. In other words, if there is a lesson to be learned from the history of art, it's that rejecting convention (art brut, musique concrète) or, on the contrary, attempting to emphasize it (collage, land art, serial music) are indistinguishable in the long run:

the only nature we see is the one the artist *decides* to let us see or hear.

This resembles the classical paradox of naturalism, in which artifice and struggle are needed for something to appear natural, all spontaneity is a construct, and the only totality is logical or cultural. For while scientists, art historians, anthropologists, and progressive politicians agree that nature, understood as a set of phenomena, is only a product of the human mind—logical, symbolic, or cultural space—they are quick to see an unchallenged nature in the universality of facts and logical or cultural structures they claim to be updating. There would be no science if the construction of facts was not considered by the scientist to be a simple reduction of phenomena to their primitive elements, independent of human activity, and therefore natural. Similarly, all art history for Panofsky, just as all anthropology for Lévi-Strauss, is haunted by a teleology that to be coherent, as is noted at the end of *The Naked Man*, should lead us to a form of naturalism whose inspiration is quasi-religious, which "places the world before life, life before man." But it is in political thought that the paradox can best be summarized: The backdrop for all political progress is a form of nature that we claim to challenge or improve in its name. If citizens are equal before the law, it is a natural law, something perfectly symbolized in the figure of Rousseau: the nostalgia of progress and the belief in man's limitless perfectibility.

## TECHNOPHOBIC ANTINATURALISM

It was to resolve this contradiction that Husserlian, then Heideggerian, phenomenology grew in popularity. If all objectivization, or construction, of a fact can claim universal status only through a process of reduction, this should be taken seriously and we must acknowledge that we can access things themselves only by revising the meaning of that reduction. Beneath all the unquestioned constructs of science and technology, we must identify the initial impetus leading to the constitution of things, of bodies, of our being-in-the-world. This means returning to the origins of geometry, to the work of art, or to political community, to understand how consciousness, our flesh-and-blood body, our being-there give meaning and presence to the things and places that surround us. From this point of view phenomenology remains embedded in an even more radical form of antinaturalism. "We are the real positivists," Husserl could claim, meaning that for him the positive order of rational science had yet to be established. What characterizes this approach is the radical reduction of all unquestioned factuality, of the "thesis of the world," that is, the naive, and barely conscious, belief in the existence of an objective world, consisting of things that exist independently of the meaning that consciousness gives them.

But in its very radicality, this antinaturalism becomes its opposite and, primarily through the Heideggerian reading of Aristotle and the pre-Socratics, rediscovers the figure of archaic Greek naturalism, one that is primary and authentic, corresponding to a life intrinsic to humans that is an extension of their fundamental or national soil (for Heidegger). Therefore, we must acknowledge, with Husserl and against Galileo, that the "Earth does not move" since it serves as the primordial soil that makes all experience possible. For Heidegger it is only through a rereading of *phusis* among the early Greek thinkers that we can reexamine our constitutive relationship with a nature that is identified with being itself. In other words, if ordinary naturalism and positivism are mistaken, it is because they present us with a nature that is, in truth, not natural, although examined, one that has been vanquished and at the same time deprived of reason through techno-scientific nonthought. In the end it is less the idea of nature that is criticized than its humanized, mechanized, technologized version, a nature deprived of meaning and the power of questioning—or thought.

It is important to understand the strength of such a position. On the one hand, it had and still has profound influence in Europe beyond the field of philosophy. Psychiatrists, poets, painters, dancers, mathematicians, politicians (from Nazis to Marxists), and ecologists (Hans Jonas) have been deeply influenced by an idea that promised to restore to nature its dimension as a fabulous problem. It is through phenomenology that we can still hope, whatever our area of specialization, to reconcile an immediate and local practice with the promise of a superhuman, cosmic universality. On the other hand, it also serves, unwillingly this time, as a warning to everyone (ecologists, artists, even scientists) that by trying to do away with the idea of nature, we risk giving in to the hopeless quest for a native soil (religious, natural, or worse), thus turning our back on scientific and technological innovation, as if phenomenology, in spite of itself, was warning us against following in its footsteps. By losing ourselves in the search for a native soil or place, or insisting that nature must be compatible with an initial meaning charged with truth, we stand a good chance of being reduced to the photographic negative of our era—militant technophobia is still a form of modernism.

## TECHNOPHILIC AND ARTIFICIALIST NATURALISM

Whether they are seen as antagonists or radical competitors, we are forced to acknowledge that between positivism and phenomenology (especially Heideggerian), contemporary European sensibility is characterized by the rejection of any simple and unequivocal relation between humans and nature.

If we were to adopt this position, however, we would over-look the fact that the old Lucretian poem, neither archaic nor postmodern (to the extent that the term has any meaning), has continued to unconsciously haunt the European conscience. Elaborating not so much a school of thought as a kind of "com-munion of saints" of nature, it has, transhistorically, been taken up successively by Spinoza in Holland, Nietzsche in Germany, Whitehead in England (and then in the United States), and Deleuze in France, and still consists in the affirmation of a na-ture that is inopportune, unequivocal, immanent, without ter-ritory, and yet arbitrary (that is, fabulous or metaphysical). It is this naturalism—necessary and arbitrary, critical and affirma-tive, that is to say, always unclean, inauthentic, hampered by technological mechanisms and imaginary projections—that we wish to draw attention to.

Nature is *inopportune*, never appropriate to its time. Nietzsche said that we can think only in opposition to our era, in the hope of a new era to come. But this incongruous thought is possible only if nature is neither denied nor forgotten but affirmed against an image of nature that restrains and vilifies it: Nature would be the physical and spiritual automatism of a life given over to itself, said Spinoza (instinctive Nietzsche called him, machinic said Deleuze). In this sense the inopportune nature of natural-ism protects us from an uncritical positivism and a nostalgia for origins: the reign of nature can never be sought in the past since it is always in the future.

Nature is *unequivocal*, is expressed as a single meaning. Such a claim signals the rejection of the opposition between nature and artifice, as well as any alternative between technicism and tech-nophobia: a recognition of the fundamental ambiguity in the idea of nature that enables us to more easily affirm it as multiple rather than as simply ambiguous. Everything is nature, every singular thing, stone or machine, expresses the same nature. From this viewpoint it is not so much a question of choosing between "protecting" nature or ignoring it, but of making it as livable as possible. Nature is neither a given (given by whom, exactly?) nor an origin or principle; it is everything that becomes. Spinoza called this "modification," Nietzsche and Deleuze called it the "being-of-becoming," Whitehead called it "process."

Nature is *immanent*. This was best expressed by Spinoza, who wrote of an immanent nature, freed of all transcendent gods and any idea of creation or finality. Without origin or end, nature is never politically anything more than what we make it, which makes impossible the development of any radical or deep ecology. All ecology is political, that is, there is no transcendent break between the natural order and the order of our technological societies.

Nature is *without territory*. This means not only that all great naturalist movements are cosmopolitan—this is their most distinctive characteristic—but also that they assume a position contrary to that of phenomenology, for which being-in-the-world means, first and foremost, being "misshapen" in the world, without ground (*ab-grund*), impure in the strict sense of the word, worried about the future and anxious about death. The absence of territory—Deleuze's *deterritorialization*—is nothing other than the Earth of life affirming that it is without foundation, without a base, or roots. To claim nature is the absence of territory is to claim a universal soil, which cannot be appropriated and is ceaselessly moving; it is to claim that uprootedness brings joy rather than anxiety—we are in nature wherever we are.

Finally, nature is *arbitrary*. This does not mean that it can be everything and anything, but that it fills a final void where any scientific explanation, any political hope, any artistic process, risks failure in its appeal to a transcendent authority (God, origin, scientific authority, the old masters) or by abandoning thought and action. Whitehead has always insisted on this point:

Nature is an arbitrary metaphysics but one that is necessary to fill in the "ultimate background" that every physical explanation requires to support its pretense to having explanatory power. Thus, nature would be, as I have indicated, a true fiction, a necessary fable, because it expresses the ultimate need of not erecting a barrier between what we think we know and what we know we don't know, between what is true and what is only hypothetical. Yet it is in this gap, this fundamental ambiguity, both recognized and rejected, that everything that is worthwhile in nature and through nature has, and will, come into being.

## BIBLIOGRAPHY

Beck, U. (1986). *La Société du risque*. Berlin.

Cassirer, E. (1927). *Individuum und Kosmos in der Philosophie der Renaissance*. Leipzig: (*The Individual and the Cosmos in Renaissance Philosophy*, translated with an introduction by Mario Domandi. Mineola, NY: Dover Publications, 2000).

——— (1932). *Die Philosophie der Aufklärung*. Berlin: (*The Philosophy of the Enlightenment* translated by Fritz C. A. Koelln and James P. Pettegrove. Boston: Beacon Press, 1955, © 1951).

Collingwood, R. G. (1945). *The Idea of Nature*. Oxford: Oxford University Press.

Deleuze, G. (1969). *Logique du Sens*. Paris: (*The Logic of Sense*, translated by Mark Lester with Charles Stivale. New York: Columbia University Press, 1990).

Deleuze, G., and Guattari, F. (1980). *Mille Plateaux*. Paris: (*A Thousand Plateaus: Capitalism and Schizophrenia*, translated by Brian Massumi. University of Minnesota Press, 1981).

Foucault, M. (1967). *Les Mots et les Choses*. Paris: (*The Order of Things: An Archeology of Human Knowledge*. New York: Vintage, 1994).

Heidegger, M. (1954).*Vorträge und Aufsätze*. Pfullinngen.

—— (1967). *Die Physis bei Aristoteles*. Frankfurt.

Jonas, H. (1979). *Das Prinzip Verantwortung*, Frankfurt.

Larrère, C. (1997). *Les Philosophies de l'Environnement*, Paris.

Latour, B. (1989). *La Science en Action*. Paris: (*Science in Action*. Cambridge, MA: Harvard University Press, 1988).

—— (1999). *Politiques de la Nature*. Paris: (*Politics of Nature: How to Bring the Sciences into Democracy*. Cambridge, MA: Harvard University Press, 2004).

Lévi-Strauss, C. (1955). *Tristes Tropiques*. Paris: (*Tristes Tropiques*, translated by John Weightman and Doreen Weightman. New York: Penguin Books, 1992).

—— (1958). *Race et Histoire*. Paris: (*Race and History*. New York: UNESCO, 1968).

—— (1972). *L'Homme Nu*. (*The Naked Man: Introduction to the Science of Mythology*, translated by John Weightman and Doreen Weightman. New York: Vintage, 1981).

Progogine, I., and Stengers, I. (1986). *La Nouvelle Alliance*. Paris.

Roupnel, G. (1966). *Histoire de la Campagne Française*. Paris.

Serres, M. (1991). *Le Contrat naturel*. Paris: (*The Natural Contract: Studies in Literature and Science*, translated by William Paulson. University of Michigan Press, 1995).

Whitehead, A. (1925). *Science and the Modern World*. New York.

—— (1929). *Process and Reality*, New York.

from India

## ON THE CONCEPT OF NATURE

———

Vinay Kumar Srivastava

**FOR ILLUSTRATING THE INDIAN** concept of nature, one may begin with the cases of communities of people (in Garhwal Himalayas, Western Rajasthan, or rural Tamil Nadu) that have made concerted efforts to preserve their respective habitats. One may also take up the examples of individuals who have done exemplary work to revive the traditional methods of eco-preservation. And one may also select a story from one of the Indian traditions that best conveys the idea of nature.

Here, I have followed the latter approach. Stories of the type I have chosen can be culled from other traditions. I submit that all these stories have a common, underlying message, which has crystallized because of the ceaseless interaction of diverse traditions from time immemorial. India is enormously diverse. At the same time, there is a subterranean unity. It is this unity that I have in mind while discussing the Indian concept of nature.

The story I have chosen is of Rām, the Vishnu-incarnated king of Ayodhyā, as narrated in the famous epic, Śrī Rāmcharitramānas.[1] Rām's wife, Sītā, a term meaning "furrow," who emerged from the earth, rather than being born of human parents, has been abducted by the ten-headed king of Lankā, Rāvan. The son of wind, the monkey-god, Hanumān, has been deputed to fetch news about the place in Lankā where Sītā has been forcibly confined. Although belonging to the genus of simians, Hanumān is not an ordinary monkey; he possesses magical qualities. For instance, in childhood, for satiating his hunger, he once devoured the sun, plunging all the three universes in unimaginable darkness, and only when the gods intervened for mercy did he release it![2] Hanumān is celibate and leads the life of an ascetic, devoting himself fully to the service of Rām.

Hanumān is endowed with supernatural athleticism. He can fly as fast as the wind; he can adopt a gargantuan shape or assume a tiny appearance; he can make his tail grow infinitely long; he can pluck an entire mountain and carry it on his palm. This amazing simian is entrusted with the task of tracing Sītā.

After overcoming initial hurdles, he reaches the lands of Lankā, adopting a frame as tiny as that of a mosquito. He moves from one place to another, seeing the demons—the residents of Lankā—gulping down buffaloes and cows, donkeys and lambs, and even humans. Amidst all this, he comes across a palace that

---

1. This story is from one of the sections of Śrī Rāmcharitramānas called Sundarkānd. Here, I have consulted its translation by Bharat Bhushan Srivastava (Tulsidas 2002b). There are many interpretations of this epic, from South Asia to Southeast Asia, but to consider them is beyond the scope of this essay.

2. See Goswami Tulsidas's Śrī Hanumān Chālīsā (Trans. Bharat Bhushan Srivastava, 2002a). The three universes are the earth (mrtyu lok), the heaven (swarga lok), and the netherworld (pātāl lok).

has a temple. On its walls are the etchings of the bow and arrow, the weapons associated with Rām, and all around it are the plants of Tulsi (basil), which are regarded as sacred.

How there could be a palace bearing sacred symbols in the lands of sullied demons bothers Hanumān until he finds out that its inhabitant, Vibhīsan by name, a younger brother of Rāvan, is an ardent devotee of Rām and has been longing to serve him. From Vibhīsan, Hanumān comes to know about the grove known as Ashok (Ashok Vātikā) where Sītā has been lodged in some kind of an open prison guarded by female demons. Rāvan visits that place in the evening, threatens to kill Sītā if she does not agree to marry him and join the harem of his wives. When Sītā refuses to even entertain this thought, he orders the female guards to frighten her mercilessly until she succumbs to his wish.

Sītā is extremely sad and depressed. She requests one of the sympathetic guards to arrange a pyre for her so that she can kill herself and be saved from the tortures to which Rāvan is subjecting her. Telling Sītā that at night no fire would be available, the guard leaves for her house. Sītā tells herself that unless she gets fire (i.e., is able to burn herself), her tribulations will not cease. She says thousands of sparks of fire appear in the sky but not even one reaches the earth. Though the moon also has fire, it does not send even a smoulder to the ill-fated woman that Sītā calls herself. Then, addressing the Ashok tree, under which she sits, Sītā says that its fresh leaves are like the flames of fire and hopes that fire will emerge from them, and before her grief multiplies, she would leave for her heavenly abode.

Perched on the branch of the tree under which Sītā moans, Hanumān drops the ring that Rām has given him to carry to Sītā as a mark of his identification. Sītā is elated on seeing it, for she knows that no power—or illusion—can create it, and hence it must have come from Rām. Then Hanumān appears before Sītā, whom he calls mother, assuring her of the tireless efforts that

Rām is making along with the army of monkeys and bears to raid the demon land and rescue Sītā. When Sītā expresses her doubt regarding the simian strength, Hanumān appears before her in his true form of a mountainous body, golden in color, an apotheosis of power and chivalry before which foes surrender forever. He also tells Sītā that monkeys are bereft of strength and wisdom, but with divine pleasure superior qualities can inhere in anyone.

Hanumān is now hungry. He is a monkey, a fact he reiterates now and then. He tells Vibhīsan in his first meeting that he does not belong to the upper social stratum (kulin); rather he is a "restless monkey, inferior in all respects." Those who recite the name of the monkey in the morning have to go without food the entire day. Seeing fruit-laden trees in Ashok Vātikā, Hanumān cannot resist his hunger, notwithstanding the fact that Sītā tells him that big warriors are keeping a watch on the garden. Hanumān is not afraid of the guards; what he beseeches is Sītā's permission, which he readily gets. In typical simian demeanor, he plucks fruits, eats some, throws others, uproots trees, and breaks branches, and the guards who try to resist him are beaten, maimed, or killed. Rāvan sends his best warriors to bring the simian under control but all in vain until Rāvan's son, Meghnād, uses an arrow infused with great supernatural power to shoot Hanumān, as a result of which the latter falls unconscious.

Tied in ropes, Hanumān is brought before Rāvan's court, which decides about the punishment to be meted out for uprooting the garden and assaulting some guards and killing others. Hanumān is a messenger from another kingdom, and messengers are not killed; therefore, the punishment Rāvan pronounces for him is to wrap rags around his tail, soak it in oil and clarified butter, and then put it on fire. Rāvan favors this punishment because he thinks that the tail is extremely dear to the monkey, and belaboring it will humble Hanumān, teaching his patrons a lesson. Hanumān's magical quality once again pre-cipitates. His tail keeps on lengthening, with the result that no cloth or greasy matter is available in the kingdom of Lankā to apply on it. Rāvan's sentinels then set fire to Hanumān's tail. Immediately Hanumān assumes a tiny form, jumping from the balcony of one building to another, setting the entire Lankā, made of gold, on fire, leaving the palace of the devotee of Rām, Vibhīsan, untouched. The author of Śrī Rāmcharitramānas, Goswāmī Tulsidās, says that the outcome of insulting an ascetic (sādhū)—and Hanumān is an ascetic—is destruction. The golden Lankā "burns like an orphan city" because of the treatment its king meted out to Hanumān.

Hanumān delivers the information about Sītā and the place where she has been kept. Now Rām and his army plan to invade Lankā, fight the race of demons, and bring Sītā back. But the major problem is that for reaching Lankā they have to cross the ocean. Vibhīsan, who has now left Lankā to seek refuge with Rām, says that although Rām's one arrow can dry up the ocean, the wisdom lies in requesting the ocean-god to suggest a way to cross it. After all, Vibhīsan reminds them, the ocean is one of the ancestors of Rām, and when requested, it would offer a vi-able suggestion. Rām accepts Vibhīsan's advice but Lakshman, Rām's younger brother, is not happy with it. He says, "My Lord! Why should we trust the god (the ocean) and try? Why not with your wrath make the ocean dry? The cowards depend on gods and fate; for divine interventions, lazybones wait."

But Rām advises Lakshman to have patience, and approaches the ocean with salutation. He spreads his prayer mat and sits on it to pray to seek the ocean's favor. Rām's prayers continue for three days but the ocean-god does not respond. Then, Rām says that without fear there is no friendship. He shall have to create fear in the mind of the ocean-god, so he asks his brother to bring his bow and arrow so that he can dry up the ocean with his fire-arrow (*agnibān*). While deciding in favor of this step, Rām says that praying before the ocean amounts to "beseeching an idiot or befriending a mischief-monger; or teaching generosity to a born miser; or talking of wisdom to a selfish man; or of dispassion to a greedy man; or having god's discourse with a lecher or angry person; these acts are as futile as sowing seeds in barren land."

Rām fixes his fire-arrow on his bow, aiming to shoot at the ocean in a fraction of a second. Soon, a blazing fire breaks out in the midst of the ocean. Crocodiles, snakes, fishes, and other sea animals are deeply perturbed. Realizing that once the fire-arrow leaves the bow nothing will be left in the ocean, the ocean-god appears before Rām in the guise of a humble Brahmin, holding in his hand a gold plate full of precious gems and jewels as a gift for Rām, for these valuables lie in the womb of the ocean. At this juncture, Kākbhusandī (the god in the morphology of crow) tells Garun (the avian-god who is the mount of Vishnu): "How much you may water a banana tree; it will bear fruits when hewed: when approached with humility, a vile fellow does not listen; he understands the language of reprimand."

The ocean-god is trembling with fear. After offering the gift to Rām, he falls at his feet and utters the following words: "Lord, please pardon me for my shortcomings; The five elements of nature—ether, fire, air, water, and earth—are dumb; with your inspiration, the illusion (*māyā*) has created them so that the world could come into existence." And if Rām wishes, the ocean-god continues, these elements will cease to exist forever. With his fire-arrow, Rām can dry up the ocean but this perhaps will not behoove his image as the creator of the universe.

Rām grants compassion to the ocean-god and asks him to suggest a way to cross the ocean. The ocean-god says, "In your army are two monkey-brothers; Nal and Nīl are their names. In their childhood, an ascetic blessed them. As a result, any heavy object they touch, including boulders and mountains, they would become light and float on water and would not sink. In this way, they will make a bridge over the ocean and your entire army will be able to cross it." But as Rām's fire-arrow has already been fixed on the bow and cannot return to its case, the ocean-god requests Rām to release it in the north where there exists a colony of the cruel people, and Rām complies. Following the ocean-god's advice, the magical monkey-brothers prepare the bridge, where on each stone is written Rām's name.

This story from Śrī Rāmcharitramānas illustrates well the Indian conception of nature, which is referred to by different terms in different Indian languages. India has more than six hundred languages and dialects, and each one of them has a different set of terms for nature. In Hindi, for instance, the term *prakartī* stands for nature; the equivalent of this word in Urdu is *kudrat*. A compound term from Urdu, such as *āb-o-hawā* (meaning "water and air") is also used colloquially for nature. Besides these, there are a host of other words, terms, and expressions that people use for conveying the idea of nature.

The English word *nature* has a group of meanings. The *Random House Dictionary of the English Language* (1983) has listed thirteen meanings of nature, of which two principally stand out. The first is that nature refers to the material world, especially that part unaffected by human activities. The second meaning of nature is the particular combination of qualities belonging to a person, animal, thing, or class by birth, origin, or constitution. As human beings are also part of nature, the word *nature* is used for their original, pristine, uncultivated, uncivilized, primitive, and wild condition. Here, nature is contrasted to culture. Nature refers to the original state, while culture consists of all those objects, material as well as nonmaterial, that human beings have created for their survival. One may understand the meaning of the term culture in the following way:

> For anthropologists (and also, sociologists) culture is the totality of living patterns of a community of human beings. Their thoughts, actions and interactions, the procedures they adopt for fulfilling their needs and wants, the meaning they subscribe to their life and its aims, the shapes of their material objects and their orientation towards them, their attitudes towards their natural environment and other communities of human beings, are all conditioned by culture, which is preeminently transmittable and acquirable. At the same time, with each generation, it undergoes qualitative and quantitative changes, serving like a sponge for several elements diffusing from the other groups of people. But culture is equally resilient; thus it resists the onslaught of many innovations that it anticipates as threatening, endeavouring its level best to maintain its identity. Since culture covers the ideas of the people, their thoughts, interpersonal relations and their creations, no discipline—particularly of social science but also perhaps of physical and biological sciences—can be oblivious to the concept of culture, although the extent to which a subject uses it will definitely vary. Economic botany uses as much the idea of culture as does the branch of pharmacology that records and investigates the people's herbal preparation. . . . For following people's knowledge of the natural phenomenon, as juxtaposed to the scientific, we need the concept of culture. Here, we may say that as the concept of zero integrates the mathematical, physical, and engineering sciences, in the same way culture integrates social, psychological, and philosophical sciences. [Srivastava 2001, p. 29]

The term *ethno-ecology* is used for the people's understanding of their natural environment, which may differ in significant terms from the scientist's (i.e., the ecologist's) understanding. In this model that contrasts nature with culture, the central idea is that human beings cannot survive in their natural state, that is, the original and the uncultivated, because the biological apparatus they are endowed with cannot ensure their livelihood. For the survival of humankind, nature is to be changed, refashioned, and harnessed to serve human needs.

And nature is transformed with the technology that human beings have created out of their imagination and thought processes. The cerebral capacity they have acquired as a culmination of their long-term evolution has made this possible. The chipping of a pebble for the first time with the explicit intention of converting it into an artifact that can work upon nature heralded the beginning of culture. All living things depend on nature for their existence, but plants and animals (barring human beings) derive their sustenance from whatever is available. They do not transform nature the way human beings have done right from the time they separated from the simian stock. Human history is a documentation of the domestication of nature, that is, exploiting nature to the fullest for the benefit of humans. In this view, nature is the womb of bounteous resources, which all organisms, irrespective of their place in the scale of evolution, use for their existence and procreation. The nature and volume of the use of resources depends on the needs of the organism. Instinctive factors determine the algebra of use in nonhumans. The concept of overuse, or what is called "over-indulgence," does not apply to them, the infrahuman world. It does not, however, imply that some animals do not indulge in destruction; monkeys are known for uprooting crops, breaking branches, and trampling young plants, as is clear from the story from Śrī Rāmcharitramānas with which this essay began. What is proposed here is the distinction between destruction and overuse; the former category may be found in the animal world but not the latter, whereas human beings are known for both destruction and overuse.

The human species—termed "man, the wise," *Homo sapiens*—is different from the other living beings in its greater ability to extract resources for its survival from nature and make them consumable. The process of the transformation of the raw into the cooked aptly distinguishes humans from other organisms. This distinction between the raw and the cooked, therefore, is structurally equivalent to the distinction between nature and culture. Animals eat raw food, while human beings process the raw into the cooked. The discovery—in fact, domestication—of fire has played the most important role in the transformation of nature. That is why it is incorrect to say that human beings are a parasite on nature. Also, humans keep improving upon their lot. They may appear to be temporarily satisfied with what is given to them, but in reality their satisfaction with the existing state of affairs is perpetually in a state of flux. They look for better resources, better technology, better governance, a better system of distribution, larger control over their environment and life, and in conclusion, all those aspects that signal their progress.

The concept of lifestyle is only applicable to humankind. Each community of people has its own lifestyle, the other term for which is *culture*. The culture of one community differs from that of another, and even when two cultures look alike, on closer inspection we may detect subtle differences between them. Enormous diversity characterizes human living. The way in which the members of a community exploit their natural resources will differ from that of others who live in the same habitat. Societies may value their past but it does not make them stationary. All human beings desire a fulfilling, disease-free, and happy existence, in which their basic needs are satisfied and they have enough resources to express themselves and their potentiality.

Lying at the core of the studies of the relationship between human beings and their habitat, this model, which has its origin in the West, proposes a dichotomy, with nature constituting one system of this interaction and humans the other. By submitting to nature, or placating it with ritual accoutrements, humans cannot overcome its ruthlessness, which is clearly witnessed in floods, earthquakes, droughts, lightning, cyclones, storms, tornadoes, and several other phenomena that have the potentiality to wipe out any evidence of life from the face of the earth. In this view, which also figures in social science textbooks, nature is symbolized as a foe that must be domesticated in a never-ending war with it. Human beings are advised to develop a technology, and continue to improve upon it, that resists the onslaught of natural fury. This view suggests that humans can occupy the summit of the hierarchy of animals when they succeed in controlling nature.[3] The terminology used to indicate a relationship with nature is from the vocabulary of conflict and attrition. Man *tames*, *enslaves*, and *humbles* nature; he *conquers* its forces; he *emerges victorious* in the *war with nature*, where presumably each of them tries to establish its superiority over the other.

Extending this analogy a little further, nature is usually conceptualized as female, whereas the conquerors of nature, the technological order and their users, are male. The idea of the social order where females are subjugated to males is extended to the relationship of human beings with nature. Nature is female, and as in the existing patriarchal order females are subordinated to males, in a similar vein nature is subordinated to the

---

3. See Srivastava (2000a) for an elaboration of this point.

designs of its exploiters, the human beings, who, with the help of culture, exploit—and often, overexploit—nature and her resources. Nature remains the silent sufferer. Incidentally, an American anthropologist, Sherry Ortner (1974), says what nature is to culture, female is to male.

The view centering on the hostility between nature and culture has come to Indians in the last century and a half, the period of their colonization. But Indian philosophy and religion do not hold the materialistic conception of nature. For them, nature is not the diametric opposite of culture; rather, nature and culture merge to form some kind of a unified system. Both human beings and nature are endowed with the same set of properties. This is clearly manifested in the episode from Śrī Rāmcharitramānas. Human beings and animals form one system, although each of these categories retains its own distinctive characteristics. Besides two humans (or better, gods incarnated as humans), Rām and his brother, the rest who constitute Rām's army are from the animal kingdom. They are bears and monkeys, which are bipeds. They speak and are intelligent. They devoutedly serve Rām not because he is human, but because he is god and whosoever serves him (whether human, demon, or animal) will get worthy release (*sadgati*) from this world and become a part of the worthy soul (*parmātmā*).

Animals share some characteristics with human beings—for instance, they want and deserve salvation—but they also have their own properties, which make them proud and give them identity. Hanumān, for instance, destroys the Ashok Vātikā by plucking fruits, of which he could have eaten a few, and uprooting trees. He does it not with the intention of teaching Rāvan a lesson, devastating his Lankā with vengefulness, because Rām has not ordered him to do that, but to indulge in this playful destruction is a part of his simian endowment. However, the same monkey is a flame of vengeance when his tail is set on fire, because the tail, as Rāvan says, is very dear to monkeys. In other words, monkeys are like humans in some respects, and in some others they have their own specific traits; yet they form a part of the greater system that includes human beings, demons, and animals.

Demons constitute one of the points of the triangle, the other two points of which are humans and animals, who come together to sound the death knell of demons. Flesh eating (including that of human beings), the demons are dark, gargantuan, cruel, and violent. By contrast, the humans (the model of whom we construct from the examples of Rām, Sītā, and Lakshman) are vegetarian (eating mainly fruits and tubers), fair in complexion, tall and slenderly built, compassionate, benevolent, and peaceful. Gods incarnate themselves in human form, but not as demons; they may, however, come to the earth in the form of animals. It is under severe provocation, such as Rāvan abducting Sītā, that they are aroused, and when this happens, the extermination of demons is certain.

As the antithesis of gods is demons, in the same way, the antithesis of human beings and animals is also demons. Humans and animals are grouped together because they provide the forms that gods take when they decide to come to the earth to liberate it from the clutches of evil. The opposition is now of human beings and animals on the one hand, and demons on the other. At the symbolic level, it in fact is the opposition of the good and bad, life and death, auspicious and inauspicious, sacred and sullied. And, when a sacred entity appears along with the defiled, it remains what it should, but has an elevation in its status. Vibhīsan, for example, is a demon in biogenetic terms, for he is Rāvan's brother, but because he has faith in Rām and craves salvation at his holy feet, he does not remain sullied. He now shares company with humans; this explains the presence of Tulsi in his palace; the sacred plant is found nowhere in

Laṅkā because its lands are polluted. But as lotus grows in mud, in the same way sacred thoughts can survive amidst an impure ambience.

All natural things are living and sensate.[4] The five elements that constitute nature are also divine, worthy of worship. The ocean, as the story from Śrī Rāmcharitramānas says, is in fact godly. When Rām urges it for help, it pays no heed, for like some people even gods may be consumed by pride. When prayers remain barren, Rām, being the supreme god and the creator of the ocean, threatens to dry it up. Confronted with Rām's wrath, the ocean-god is without any option except to make an appearance before Rām, apologize profusely, and suggest the way of crossing. Others presumably do not know what the ocean-god suggests, irrespective of the fact that the members of the simian army have been living with Nal and Nīl for quite sometime, and they eventually build the bridge over the ocean to reach Laṅkā. Devotees returning from Rāmesh-varam, from where the bridge was built to Laṅkā, claim to have seen the pebbles, the remnants of the bridge, that still float in the ocean.

The story from Śrī Rāmcharitramānas shows that the assumed contrast—or opposition—between nature and culture is not really universal. The story discussed here to illustrate this point is from a Hindu epic, as I noted in the beginning of this essay, but stories of a similar content and themes can be found in other

---

4. One of the Urdu verses expresses this idea lucidly:

Rakh qadam phūnk phūnk kar nādān,
Zarre zarre mein jān hei pyāre.
(Oh, dear simpleton! Take care with each of your steps,
For each bit, each speck is lifeful.)

traditions and religious communities. India is multicultural. Notwithstanding the apparent differences between cultures, one unmistakably discovers cultural unity in India, which has historically resulted from the processes of borrowing, accommodation, and assimilation of cultural traits. External influences emanating from towns and cities, the centers of great tradition, have been able to change even the remotely placed tribal societies, such as in northeast India, believed to be away from the hub of civilization. And the communities of the great tradition have also appropriated ideas from tribal and peasant communities. Because both these processes have been at work from time immemorial, one discovers cultural unity in India and also in much of South Asia.[5]

To reiterate, the idea held in traditional India is that all objects of the nonhuman world are endowed with life, including the boulders and mountains that stand unmoved for millennia. Many of these objects in the other systems of thought are unambiguously regarded as nonliving. The presence of life in everything makes the things sensitive to the world around them. They experience pain and pleasure, grief and happiness. They also speak, that is, communicate in their own way, and establish one-to-one relationships with individuals. Some of these things are regarded in certain religious systems as godly entities themselves or as the abodes of deities and spirits, because of which they are worthy of veneration as the divine element dwells in them. They are also intelligent. If need be, they advise human beings and others wisely. A cursory reading of the classical text, *Panchtantra*, will apprise the reader of the pearls of wisdom contained in the speeches of animals and birds. Therefore, one should have respect for the entire creation.

---

5. In traditional India, tribal communities have not been isolated from the communities of peasants and town dwellers. See Mehra (1987, pp. 35–41).

The world surrounding human beings is quite like the human world, but then each species has its own properties. It is possible that one may be transmuted into the other. One of the instances in the story of Rām points out that a rock (shilā) may in fact be a woman who becomes so because of the curse of an ascetic. When Rām accidentally tumbles over it, the rock is transformed into a woman as a result of the divine touch. Stories of this kind can be gleaned from the other traditions as well. The point is that different species in the universe are in a relation of interdependence. Each is bestowed with its own characteristics, as was said earlier, although they all share certain common traits that are fully developed in the case of human beings. The monkeys and bears in Rām's army wear loincloths, jewels, and headgear, stand erect, speak, and are well trained in techniques of warfare, but their typical characteristics continue to exist. This would explain why Hanumān tells time and again that as a monkey he is restless and indulges in destruction.

Then, what, according to Indians, is nature made up of? One may catalogue a number of things that constitute nature, such as air, heat, water, clouds, earth, celestial bodies, underearth, and netherworld, myriad resources that lie buried, innumerable species of plants and animals, humans included. For Indians, nature is not something outside them. Both the words prakarti and kudrat mean the entire creation, which includes the human species as well. Not only are human beings a part of nature, it is also within them. They are as much an embodiment of nature as are the other things, living or nonliving, moving or stationary. But human beings are different from the other species because of their larger ability to reflect on reality and create abstract thoughts. The Indian thought unequivocally submits that all entities are sensate—able to think and feel—but human beings are placed at the summit of the hierarchy of all things because they excel in this property that they have acquired as a result of their evolution (*pragati*) and, as religious thoughts would say, the blessings of divinity.

Like human beings anywhere in the world, Indians also believe that whichever thing they need for their ongoing existence and nurturance comes from nature. Plants give them food, fodder, wood, and medicines; animals give them food, wool, milk, leather, traction power, and fuel; the sun gives them light and energy; the clouds give them water; and so on. But for Indians, it is myopic—in fact, irreligious—to view nature as a mere repository of resources, exploited, often overexploited, for the life and the unlimited comforts of humans and their burgeoning population. Nature is symbolized as female, but not just as female to be mastered by her male counterpart, symbolized in the form of culture. She is the mother, the bountiful mother goddess, who feeds the numerous inhabitants of earth as her own children.[6] In the event of the shortage of resources, or floods and droughts, people urge compassion upon nature. Confronting it with an armory of technology is completely ruled out. In traditional religion, nature is worshiped in a variety of forms: the rivers are goddesses; trees are abodes of supernatural forces as well as, for some of them, the deities themselves; the natural entities are divine beings; the sun and the moon are gods themselves; some animals and birds are also symbols of gods and goddesses. Lord Krishna, an incarnation of Vishnu, says in Bhagavad Gita: "Of lights I am the radiant sun; Among the stars I am the moon; Of the bodies of water I am the ocean; Of immovable things I am the Himalayas; Of all trees I am the banyan

---

6. After the devastating earthquake in Gujarat on 26 January 2001, a number of poems appeared in Hindi magazines and those of regional languages, which questioned the motherly role of the earth. The role of the mother is to nurture her children and not cause death to them.

tree; Among the beasts I am the lion; Of fishes I am the shark; Of flowing rivers I am the Ganges!"[7]

A widely held belief among Hindus is that the tree of Pipal (*Ficus religiosa*) is sacred, for it is the dwelling of Lord Shiva as well as the members (*gana*) of his entourage, the ghosts and goblins (*bhūt pret*). Under the shade of this tree, temples are invariably built up. Even when it does not have a temple underneath, people light a lamp at its foot, make offerings of food, clothes, and money, and the devout ones may sit under it in meditative repose and pray. The tree itself becomes the temple. In some parts of India, the same sentiments are built around the banyan tree (*Ficus bengalensis*).[8]

The plant of Tulsi is also regarded as a personification of divinity, as was observed earlier. Certain Indian communities have the tradition of keeping Tulsi in the courtyard. They also periodically arrange the marriage of this goddess with Saligram, a male deity who is symbolized by a black, round stone, which is always kept in the plant of Tulsi. A bright-colored, heavily embroidered wrap covers Tulsi, indicating her marital status, and this would also explain why only married women are permitted to conduct her worship, although unmarried girls and widows can always stand before her and pray. In the Himalayas, where Tulsi is unable to withstand the chilly weather and the plant withers away, the people collect its seeds, keep them in a safe place, and grow the plant at the onset of the suitable climate. However, the pot in which Tulsi grows is also an object of veneration. When there is no plant, as is the case during win-

---

7. All these statements are from Chapter 10 of Bhagavad Gita.

8. I want to point out here that the question of origin and evolution of these beliefs is not taken up in this essay, for it cannot be answered satisfactorily in the absence of reliable data about nonmaterial cultural facts from prehistoric times.

ters, the belief is that the pot in which it grows is equally sacred and worshipable. One of the popular television serials in Hindi, titled *Kyunki Sas Bhi Kabhi Bahu Thi*, has strongly reinforced the cult of Tulsi.

Like plants and trees, many Indian communities regard certain animals as the symbols of gods and goddesses. Rats, for example, are venerated in a temple of the mother goddess known as Karnī Mātā, the clan-goddess of the Rajputs of Bikaner, situated at Deshnoke (Rajasthan). The compound of this temple has thousands of well-fed rats, which are in abundance in the sanctum sanctorum. Devotees feed the rats with sweetmeats and wait anxiously for a glance (*darsana*) of the white-colored rat, for it is auspicious and foretells a bright future for those who spot it. Similarly, the bird with a blue neck (known as *nīlkanth*) is believed to be a symbol of Lord Shiva. The latter also has a blue neck because he drank the bowl of poison (*vish*) that had emerged from the sea after the gods and demons jointly churned it. As someone was expected to drink it, the churners turned to Lord Shiva as he is reputed to consume intoxicants and poisonous weeds (*dhatūrā*). Shiva knew that if the poison went inside his body he would die, so he stored the poison forever in his throat, as an outcome of which his neck became blue. A common practice in North India is that on the day of Shiva worship (called Shiva Rātrī), bird catchers roam the streets with caged *nīlkanth*. The cage is covered with a piece of cloth; it is taken inside the house, its cover is taken off, and the devotees are permitted to have a glimpse. An offering of money or of certain things in kind (*dakshinā*) is made to the bird. To have a glance of the blue-neck bird on Shiva Rātrī is taken as boon granting!

Mountains are also regarded as sacred and divine dwellings. Gobardhan, a mountain in Mathura, is believed to have been touched by Lord Krishna. He held it on the tip of his index finger, thus making space for people to stand under it with their families and animals, so that they could escape from the devastating fury of rains that had been sent by Lord Indra, the god of rains, who could not reconcile himself to the fact that with the rise of Krishna-worship, devotion to him was fast receding. Today, devotees circumambulate Gobardhan; some do it prostrating, and some walk on their knees. The number of rounds they take depends on their wish or the vow they have taken; some are content with one round, while some move around the sacred mountain 108 times, as this is regarded a sacred number, or even more! The more one subjects one's body to sufferings, the more are the chances of attaining spiritual heights! The Mount Kailash, believed to be Shiva and his consort's abode, is another site of pilgrimage for Hindus, regardless of the fact that it is one of the most arduous and expensive journeys. It is important to note that in contemporary India, with the rise of Hindu-consciousness (or political Hinduism, what is called Hindutva), Kailash pilgrimage (known as Kailash Mānsarovar Yātrā) has acquired immense popularity and one can imagine the negative effects of religious tourism on fragile ecosystems.

Against this background, one may appreciate the Indian belief that nature gives all means and wherewithal—and has the infinite ability to give more and more—because it is a personification of divinity. When it is annoyed, it can unleash unimaginable terror to remind its exploiters (or those who mortify it) of its measureless prowess. Sunderlal Bahuguna (1986), a noted environmentalist from the Himalayas, wrote:

Be it the death of trees or collective death of human beings as in Bhopal, or slow death of millions due to air and water pollution and desertification, the causes of these are in human beings' misbehaviour with nature. Glorified as development, it is born from the conception that Man is the Master of Nature. [p. 5]

Or, as a noted writer, Khushwant Singh (2002), said, "Trees contribute everything they have; humans only know how to take all they can from the soil, foul the atmosphere and give nothing in return."

But humans soon realize that they are not the masters of the universe when ecological crises start surfacing. When the monsoon is delayed, people in villages and towns seek its cause in their bad behavior, declining morality, and the lowering of their respect for nature. A number of fire-oblation ceremonies (havan, yagya) are organized all over India for placating nature for good rains. Several local rituals are held for the same purpose. For instance, in Vadodara (Gujarat), elephants are bathed; in Ahmedabad (Gujarat), leaders of peasant communities forsake food; in towns of Rajasthan, holy litany (mantra) from the Vedas is chanted. In Pali-Marwar (Rajasthan), it is believed that if a widow cries all alone in a secluded place and requests Lord Indra to grant rain, it will come. In Udaipur (Rajasthan), people roll boulders from hillocks, assuming that rains will follow the thunderous sound. In Allahabad (Uttar Pradesh), village boys smeared with mud pray for rain. In Delhi, a famous dancer performs a dance performance from Bhāratnātyam to invoke the rain god. In south Rajasthan, the tribals believe that merchants magically stop rains because they profit most in a drought.[9] People would approach them for loans of money and grains, and this is the reason for frequent attacks on merchants and their holy men. One of the rituals that has come up in this part of Rajasthan is that the merchants are asked to stand with an earthen pitcher filled with water on their heads while a tribal member shoots the pitcher with an arrow. The breaking of the pitcher with water spilling all over is believed to nullify the magical spells that may

9. See Srivastava (2000c).

arrest rains. Then, one also comes across a violinist playing a tune (*rāga*) that "melts the heart of nature"! The point is that even when people know how clouds are formed and why rain comes, they also believe that as nature creates itself, as it is sui generis, it is all-powerful and decides about the fate of various phenomena. People have no alternative but to submit before nature with words like these:

> Allah! Send us rainbearing clouds; Give us water;
> Shyam! The world waits for your benevolence;
> Ram! Our hope is our faith in you;
> Allah! Send us rain.[10]

Here, we contrast the Eastern and the Western notions of nature. In simple terms, materialism reigns in the West, whereas spiritualism is the core value of the East. In the West, science developed independently of religion, and was regarded (and is still regarded) as the antithesis of religion and spirituality. By comparison, in the East, science is integrated with religion; therefore, it is unsurprising to come across scientists of eminence observing rituals and nurturing their faith in their respective religions. These perspectives of materialism and spiritualism are respectively extended to nature, as they envelop the other spheres of social living. If for the West nature is a soulless mine of assets, for the East it is a living entity, with feelings and sensations, whose ability to generate resources of all types is beyond our imagination. Nature's secrets and laws are fully knowable, so assert Western scientists, and once we have the specialized technology, we shall be in a position to know the causes of various

---

10. This is an English translation of the lines from a song in a Hindi film titled *Guide*.

phenomena and control them. On the other hand, Eastern philosophers submit that nature reveals what she wants to and she herself decides which secrets of hers are to be exposed and in what measure, and which of them should remain concealed for the time being.

The predictions of natural phenomena and their behavior often fail because one perhaps cannot fully grasp the designs of nature. Howsoever optimistic one may be in scientific terms, one shall never succeed in mastering nature, so believe the people from India. Furthermore, whenever humans have boasted of their knowledge of nature and acquiring mastery over her, they have encountered her insuperable wrath. Notwithstanding their claim of knowledge of natural phenomena, the people and the life on the planet have perished in earthquakes, floods, droughts, landslides, cyclones, avalanches, and several other natural catastrophes. Indian philosophy expresses the lacunae of the view that humans are the masters of nature, suggesting that the chief good of the human species lies in cultivating a reverential attitude toward nature. One discovers in Indian philosophy and thought an intimate relationship between religion and environment. Religion safeguards the environment, thereby guaranteeing its healthy perpetuation.

The spiritual and respectful attitude toward nature has gained ascendancy in several environmental movements that have surfaced in the last three to four decades. Besides this, several religious movements have also adopted a more spiritualistic view of nature.[11] This may be illustrated with the case of the movement of white witchcraft (or modern witchcraft) that has now

---

11. For instance, many Buddhist organizations committed to environmental protection emphasize that the principles needed for this work, for making people become "better stewards of the planet," are of "nonviolence, tolerance, self-awareness, and compassion for other living beings" (Powers 1995).

become quite popular in the West.[12] In recent years, it has also spread to Eastern countries as well. India has the distinction of having a person, known as Ipsita Roy Chakraverty, who has made her proud commitment to modern witchcraft public. She claims that the source of her creativity, for she is a painter and writer of repute, is traced to witchcraft.[13] Those who adhere to modern witchcraft regard it as a full-fledged religion; for them, because white witchcraft is a religion, like other institutionalized religions, it should be written with capital W's.[14] Although sharing a common name, different groups (or covens, as they are called) paying allegiance to white witchcraft do not have a uniform body of rituals and ideological principles. Each group improvises its own battery of rituals and thoughts, which it does by borrowing from a variety of religions and belief systems of the world (particularly Indian) and then accommodating (or syncretizing) the borrowed stuff to its fundamental principles.

However, a belief that different covens of witches share, which are also sometimes antagonistically placed, is that they all want to revive the pre-Christian religion that was natural, that is, it drew upon natural forces and approached them for help and mercy. This nature-worshiping religion was purged with the advent of Christianity. With the passage of time, the state exterminated its practitioners with severe punishments pronounced for them. As a result, the followers of white witchcraft believe, human beings were alienated from nature, viewing it as a ruth-

---

12. It is also called the Wiccan (see Farrar and Farrar 1987); for an anthropological analysis of modern witchcraft, see Srivastava (1988, 1989) and Luhrmann (1989).

13. See Roy Chakraverty (1996); also see an article about a workshop on occult healing that Roy Chakraverty conducted in Kolkata in 1990 (Sarma 1990).

14. See Farrar and Farrar (1987).

less force that had to be reined technologically. Emphasis was laid, therefore, on developing the technology of control rather than drawing closer to nature to seek its blessings and favor. As people return to the nature-worshiping religion, the worship of the earth, the mother earth, which white witchcraft respectfully terms *gaia*, becomes central to their system.[15]

The witches, as the members of the modern witchcraft call themselves, are particularly conscious of the fact that unabated industrialization and people's insatiable desire to explore all the secrets of nature have led to irreparable damage to the earth and her resources. The earth reacts to this situation by reminding people of her uncontrollable powers expressed through the eruption of volcanoes, inordinate delays in the monsoon, djinn-like powerful cyclones and tornadoes, and massive earthquakes.

Against this background, the witches believe in performing rituals that have the effect of healing the earth, pacifying its anger, rejuvenating its powers, and seeking its blessings. The earth-healing ritual varies from one coven to another, for each improvises what it supposes would be the best, but the explicit aim of the ritual remains the same. On the earth-healing day, the witches assemble in an open space, preferably a site of the natural landscape, so that they are as close to nature as is possible, conduct the ritual they have collectively designed, and chant to heal the earth.[16] One of the chants that I collected during my fieldwork with witches in England proceeded in the following way:

---

15. In one of the articles on modern witches, they were described as fierce environmentalists (Nance 1989).

16. In many covens, the witches perform their rituals in the nude. One of the reasons they give is that when they are without clothes, or scantily dressed, they absorb more of natural power, as clothes alienate human beings from nature and her energy (Farrar and Farrar 1987).

Wake the flame inside us, burn and burn below,
Fire seed and fire feed, and make the magic grow.

Shout unto our inner selves, men and women all,
Open up your inner ears, so we may hear the call.
Wake the flame inside us, burn and turn without,
Fire seed and fire feed, and squeeze the poison out.

The silent scream of dolphins, the long dark wall
of earth,
The thrashing of a poisoned sea, the silence of
stillbirth,
The creeping poison in the air, the acid in the rain,
Corrosion in the soul of greed, the fever in the
brain.

We call to you from north and south, to come to
us this hour,
And east and west to join us, with your strength
and might and power.
Wake the flame inside us, burn now and without
end,
Fire seed and fire feed, and make the earth to mend.

It is clear that the witches refer to the destruction of nature in recent times and pray for resurrection of the natural equilibrium in their chants and prayers. They also refer to the greed that has overtaken human beings, because of which they unleash unimaginable and irreversible terror in the environment. When this environmental ethics returns to India, even under the cover of witchcraft, which has been a tabooed category, almost a horror, it will be readily accepted because Indians have always looked at nature spiritually and respectfully.

This section, describing how some religions in India have conceptualized and treated nature, is a further elaboration of the idea that nature is a spiritual entity. It should be worshiped, venerated, and respected, and human beings should be eternally grateful to it because it ensures their survival.

For Hindus, the divinity is one that has myriad forms, apparently one different from the other, but they all dissolve into one. The idea that God pervades each minuscule part of the universe (*kan kan mein bhagwān*), for He is the creator, is common to all texts, and also to past and contemporary communities. One of the incarnations of Vishnu, Lord Krishna, says, "I am the father of this universe, the mother, the support and the grandsire. I am the object of knowledge, the purifier and the syllable Om. I am also the Rg, the Sāma and Yajur Vedas" (Bhagavad Gita 9:17). Further, he describes himself as "pervading everything of the universe" (*sarvam āvrtya tisthati*): "Everywhere are His hands and legs, His eyes, heads and faces and He has ears everywhere. In this way the supersoul exists, pervading everything" (Bhagavad Gita 13:14).

In other texts, entities such as ether, air, fire, water, earth, planets, all creatures, directions, plants and trees, rivers, oceans, and mountains and hills are considered as different organs of the God's body. Worshiping these entities implies God's worship. One does not see God through normal senses. For this, one has to perform severe austerities and penances. But what one sees are the creations and manifestations of God; therefore, one is advised to hold everything of nature, including lowly, sickly, leprous, and despicable human beings, in reverence. A pundit (erudite scholar) is defined in the Bhagavad Gita (5:18) in the following words: he is a humble sage who by virtue of true knowledge sees "with equal vision" a learned and gentle Brahmin, a cow, an elephant, a dog, and an outcaste.

According veneration to everything of nature also means that for the Hindu thought, God (*parmatmān*) and nature (*prakarti*) are interchangeable categories. Not only is the element (*ansh*) of God in everything, God has also appeared on the earth in the form of animals. When He appeared in anthropomorphic form, He displayed exceptional love for animals. God has incarnated Himself as a fish (*matsya*), tortoise (*kachuā*), boar (*bārah*), and half-man and half-lion (*narsingh*). In the form of Ram, as we have seen earlier, He had close association with monkeys and bears, and as Krishna, He was a cow herder.

This further supports the point that although animals and humans are different, they share the same essence. One can be transformed into the other and they can work cooperatively on a mission. The respect accorded to animals can be gauged from the practice Hindus observe at funeral rituals and those conducted to commemorate the memory of the dead. Before their priests eat on these occasions, morsels of food cooked for feeding the dead are served to the crow, the dog, and the cow. In these rituals, priority is accorded to the animal world over that of humans.

The attitude Hindus have toward animals legitimizes vegetarianism, at least in theory, if not in practice, because there are Hindu communities, some of them of Brahmins, reputed for eating flesh, and some of them regard eggs and fish as examples of vegetarian food, a classification that cannot go unchallenged. The animals have life and experience pain. With respect to them, human beings should unflinchingly adhere to the doctrine of nonharming (*ahimsā*). Before inflicting pain on anyone, humans should imagine themselves as being placed in the other's place, for the experience of pain is identical to all beings.

Of all the species in the world, human beings are the only ones who can indulge in wanton destruction and commit acts of demerit (*adharmic kārya*). Nature has not given humans any duties or instinctive actions that remain unchanged, as is the case with plants and animals. For instance, it is in the nature of the scorpion to bite, or the lion to kill other animals for its food, or the rose to have thorns. The story of an ascetic who tried to save a scorpion from being swept away by strong tides is well known. He brought the scorpion out of water with his hands, when it stung him. A layperson was observing this. He could not resist asking the ascetic why he saved the scorpion when he knew full well that it would bite him. The ascetic's answer was that it was his duty (*dharma*) to save the dying scorpion and it was the scorpion's duty to sting. Each one lives according to its nature.

Because humans do not have a predetermined nature, they may kill barbarously and they may also render unparalleled compassion to others. Therefore, it has been imperative for every culture to define the duties according to which its members will live, and one of them is that they will regard all beings inhabiting the earth (the mother earth) as constituting an extended family, the idea of *vasudhā kutumbakam*, that the entire world (the earth) is a *kutumb* (extended family). For the continuity of a family, the functional requirements are love and concern for all. In the same way, the universe will survive if human beings nurture love for all beings and put it into practice.

Human beings are expected to guarantee a fearless existence to all beings, the idea conveyed by the concept of *abhaydān* (the "unreturnable donation of fearlessness"). Only by living in harmony with nature will humans achieve peace and a continuity of their kind. This idea is well developed in Buddhism and Jainism. In Buddha's life, nature enters as an important, positive force. Gautam, who after his enlightenment became the Buddha, was born under a tree. When he took his first steps, lotus flowers blossomed. As a child, he often meditated under trees and it was under a Bodhi tree that he was enlightened. The first sermon he delivered was in an animal park. Similarly, the

Jains believe that when Mahāvīr, their twenty-fourth ford maker (tirthānkara), meditated, animals of different predispositions and nature—some carnivorous, others herbivorous, some ferocious, some docile, animals that have a predatory relationship with others—sat around him giving up their respective characteristics. All this constituted an "assembly of listeners," a body that is cardinal to Jainism.[17] Not only Mahāvīr, but also other ford makers of Jainism have meditated in the company of animals. A picture of a recent Jain renouncer, Shri Shānti Sūrī-jī Mahārāj, whose temple is at Mandoli (Jalore, Rajasthan), shows him in a cataleptic state of meditation, with all types of animals seated around him. The caption of this picture is: "The World is One."[18]

Both Buddhism and Jainism prescribe numerous injunctions against actions that may destroy nature. Killing or injuring living beings is regarded as fundamentally immoral, with terrible consequences in this and future lives. Hindu scriptures carry detailed accounts of the hells in which the violators of religious and moral injunctions are liable to languish. Jains believe that one must endeavor not to harm living beings. It is not only that they practice vegetarianism, which for them also includes not eating those vegetables that grow under the soil, but refrain from killing insects, mosquitoes, or bugs, knowing full well that their bites may cause serious ailments to human bodies. Even sexual intercourse is viewed as a violent act causing the annihilation of microorganisms that dwell in and around the genitalia (Jaini 1991). One should, therefore, indulge in sex with the explicit intention of procreation, not pleasure-seeking.

The ideology of nonharming, which emerged in Hinduism, received further reinforcement from Buddhism and Jainism. It launched a frontal attack on the ritual of blood sacrifice that many

---

17. See Carrithers and Humphrey, eds. (1991) and Laidlaw (1995).

18. See Srivastava (1997).

communities had been conducting to pacify their punitive and blood-thirsty deities. While certain tribal societies sacrificed fowls, in many Hindu temples, especially those patronized by martial groups (such as Rajputs) or housing deities that demanded blood sacrifice, lambs and buffaloes were regularly slaughtered to placate the powers. On record are the Jain ascetics who exhorted the priests officiating at blood sacrifice to stop it or replace it with that of a surrogate (say, a vegetable). There were ascetics, from different religious streams, who argued that the best sacrifice was of one's own self, and the path to achieve it was renunciation (samnyāsa). By sacrificing animals or killing them for food, one accumulated demerits (pāp), which would determine one's future births, whether as human or some lowly placed animal or insect. Hinduism believes that there are 8.4 million species (jonī), placed in a hierarchy, the apex of which is occupied by humankind, and the species in which a soul will be born depends on one's actions in this birth. The higher the demerits, the higher are one's chances of an inferior birth.

The outcome of these movements that tried to spread the values of vegetarianism and the exhortations of ascetics and holy men has been that many temples and communities have replaced animal sacrifice by that of a surrogate. I have come across temples where lemons, cucumbers, betel nuts, and coconuts are offered as sacrificial objects instead of live animals; however, the sequence of sacrificial rituals remains the same.

In Jainism, plants as well as animals are deemed to share certain characteristics with human beings. In common with animals and humans, plants have a form of consciousness and awareness of their surroundings. They also have, according to Jains, a "sense of both fear and possession" (Dundas 1992, pp. 90–91). Further, the plants are capable of perfecting them spiritually, first being born as sacred trees and then subsequently progressing to human birth. Compared to plants, animals have five senses and a certain degree of discrimination. They are also capable of remembering their previous existences. Also, they can modify their normal patterns of behavior, and progress further in the scale of spirituality.

Islam submits that God (Allah) has created everything in this universe in due proportion; therefore, each of His creations has a particular function to perform. Because of the fact of creation, "Allah hath power over all things."[19] He has "made the earth your couch, and the heavens your canopy; and sent down rain from the heavens; and brought forth therewith fruits for your sustenance."[20] Everything that Allah has created provides ample signs of His existence, and each entity is for the profit of human beings, as is clear from the following passage:

> Behold! In the creation of the heavens and the earth; in the alternation of the Night and the Day; in the sailing of the ships through the Ocean for the profit of mankind; in the rain which Allah sends down from the skies, and the life which He gives therewith to an earth that is dead; in the beasts of all kinds that He scatters through the earth; in the change of the winds, and the clouds which they trail like their slaves between the sky and the earth;— [here] indeed are the signs for a people that are wise.[21]

Allah has provided the sustenance for everyone: "So eat and drink of the sustenance provided by Allah and do no evil nor mischief on the [face of the] earth."[22] All things that God has created are expected to serve Him, which means obeying the commandments that He has pronounced.

---

19. The Holy Qur'an, Al-Baqarah: 20.
20. The Holy Qur'an, Al-Baqarah: 22.
21. The Holy Qur'an, Al-Baqarah: 164.
22. The Holy Qur'an, Al-Baqarah: 60.

Human beings, animals, and plants possess the same essence, because all of them have been created from water: "And Allah has created every animal from water: of them there are some that creep on their bellies; some that walk on two legs; and some that walk on four."[23] Animals and the other living beings are like the communities of human beings: "There is not an animal [that lives] on the earth, nor a being that flies on its wings, but [forms part of] communities like you."[24] Some chapters in the Qur'an are named after animals and insects, such as Al-Baqarah (Chapter 2, The Heifer or The Cow), An-Nahl (Chapter 16, The Bee), An-Naml (Chapter 27, The Ant), and Al-Ankabut (Chapter 29, The Spider).

But there is a hierarchy of the living beings in which humankind is placed above all, because "he alone is gifted with rational faculties and spiritual aspirations as well as power of action" (Usman 2001, p. 27). According to the Qur'an, humans are God's "vicegerent on earth," His "noblest creation" (Usman 2001, p. 252). Because of the status that humans enjoy, their responsibility toward the other creatures of the world also increases. Although God has created animals primarily for the benefits of human beings, He has demanded from them certain obligations and duties. For instance, Islam has strictly prohibited infliction of torture on animals, or playing with their lives for fun or sport (as in hunting, bullfighting, cockfighting). Islamic laws forbid vivisection on live animals or dismembering their bodies. Prophet Muhammad has declared that it is a great sin to imprison animals, pinion them for target shooting, beat them, brand them on their faces, kill nonpoisonous snakes, or use the skin of wild animals. In other words, Islam lays "great emphasis on animal rights and man's responsibility for their welfare" (Usman 2001, p. 123).

23. The Holy Qur'an, An-Nur: 45; also see Al-Anbiya: 30.
24. The Holy Qur'an, Al-Anam: 38.

There are several instances from the life of Prophet Muhammad that show his concern for the environment and its proper management, besides the compassion that he showered upon animals and plants. The Prophet said, "If any Muslim plants a tree or raises a field, and a human, bird, or animal eat from it, it shall be reckoned as charity from him."[25] He also said that for kindness shown to living creatures, there would be a "meritorious award." Once he narrated a story of compassion to his companions. On a day of hot summer, a prostitute passed by a dog that was lying hungry and thirsty, panting, and looked almost dead. She was overwhelmed with kindness, took off her stockings, tied them with her headdress, dipped it in a well, and dropped water in the dog's mouth. For that action of hers, God "forgave all her sins" (Usman 2001, p. 123). A man had taken away the nestlings of a bird, which the Prophet ordered him to return from where he had got them because the mother would be waiting for her babies (Siddiqui 2002). Once the Prophet saw an emaciated camel, whose "back had shrunk to its belly." At that time, he said that men should ride the beasts in "good weather and free them for work while they are still in good health" (Usman 2001, p. 123).

Regarding the environmental ethics, certain aspects are of tremendous importance from the tradition of the Prophet: for example, water resources should not be polluted; pathways and shades should not be rendered dirty; trees that give shelter to travelers and animals should not be felled; water, pasture, and fire should be shared by all people; water should not be wasted even when it may be plentifully available; one should plant saplings, even on the impending Day of Judgment, for this will be rewarded.

A cumulative outcome of these prescriptions is the protection and conservation of the environment, which ensures one's own

---

25. Quoted by Siddiqui (2002, pp. 74–75).

survival, the survival of all living beings, and posterity. The responsibility of humans in safeguarding the environment is great, because they are the heirs to the world that God has created. Human beings are responsible for all the harmful consequences that follow. It is because they have the potentiality to squander resources, bring corruption on earth, and exterminate life from the planet. If they do so, they will be singing their funeral ode. Islam holds that being God's vicegerents on earth, human beings have to protect the natural environment that God has created. S. H. Nasr has succinctly expressed the Islamic idea in the following words: "No peace [is] possible among men unless there is peace and harmony with nature. . . . He who is at peace with God is also at peace with His creation, both with nature and with men."[26]

The idea of environmental conservation, protecting it from degradation, figures in all religious systems in India, which earnestly advise their adherents to opt for a simple, moderate living, couched in the idiom of respect for all things that constitute nature, living and nonliving. Some religions may not directly address the issues of ecology, but their maxims and precepts definitely have a bearing on nature. It is because all religions and philosophies realize that human beings exist in the lap of nature. If nature is devastated, there will be no question of the survival of humankind. It is imperative, therefore, that humans adopt a nonexploitative, nonaggressive, noncommercial, and gentle attitude toward nature, regarding it as their lifeline. How human beings should deal with nature may be learned, as Buddhists say, from the analogy of a bee, which collects pollen grains from flowers without jeopardizing their beauty or fragrance. The ball is in the court of humankind, which has to judiciously devise methods to derive resources from nature without causing its despoliation.

---

26. Quoted by Usman (2001, p. 165).

The religious ideas concerning the meaning of environment and how it should be protected have funneled down to different Indian communities. There are several examples of communities that have consciously tried to protect their environment. One comes across people from different walks of life who lead a frugal living, not because they are poor, but because it is their cultural pattern. This type of living has definite unintended consequences for environmental protection and its growth. Oft quoted is Mahatma Gandhi's famous statement that earth produces enough to fulfill the needs of all beings but certainly it cannot satiate the greed and avarice of humans, who are solely responsible for destructions all around.

This section discusses the attempts that small communities have made to protect their environment.

There are cases of communities in India that have included aspects of environmental protection and regeneration in the charter of principles their members are expected to follow. For instance, the Raikas of Rajasthan, a community of sheep and camel breeders, have a set of ten principles (which they call *dharma*), of which the third principle is *badlo kātan nāye*, meaning not to ax or fell the banyan tree.[27] The term used here is *badlo* (banyan), implying that the Raikas have a special, reverential relationship with this tree, but the Raikas say that they extend these sentiments to all trees. Being pastoral, they say their animals depend on green leaves and grasses rather than wood, and if trees disappear, it will be their and their animals' doomsday.

The Raikas's fourth principle is *pīpal pujan jāye*, meaning they should worship the Pipal tree (*Ficus religiosa*). As this tree is regarded as the abode of Lord Shiva, and Monday happens to be the day when he is worshiped, Pipal is also worshiped on Mon-

---

27. For a discussion of these principles, see Srivastava (2000b).

day. In those areas of Rajasthan where Pipal is not available, the Raikas worship another tree called Khejri (*Prosopis*). According to some Raikas, Khejri is the Tulsi of the deserts of Rajasthan. The third principle may advise people not to cut any tree, with the word *badlo* standing as a symbol of vegetation in general rather than exclusively for banyan, but the fourth principle does not advise the worship of every tree. The seventh principle of the Raikas prohibits the sale of the milk of their animals. Often, the Raikas say that selling of milk is almost like selling of one's children. This principle acts against the consideration of their animals (and their products) as commercial things. Now, in some parts of Rajasthan, this principle is not strictly adhered to because of the impact of the nongovernmental organizations that are inspiring the Raikas to sell milk and augment their income. But still, they do not treat their animals (and their products) as commercial entities, as is the case with several agro-pastoral communities whose life is considerably dependent on the sale of milk.

Another community of Rajasthan and Haryana, well documented in literature for protecting their environment, is of the Bishnois, who claim to follow their own religion, and that is why they may be considered as an example of a religious community. Some writers and environmentalists think that the movement to save nature by "hugging trees" originally emerged with the Bishnois in the first half of the eighteenth century. However, the same movement in the Himalayas in the twentieth century, which earned the name of Chipko ("to hug"), might be an independent development. These thinkers do not suggest the diffusion of the movement from Rajasthan to the Himalayas. What they essentially argue is that one of the ways of saving the trees from being felled is by hugging them, and the Bishnois of a village now called Khejarli accidentally discovered this way in A.D. 1730 when 363 men, women, and children sacrificed their lives saving Khejri trees from being felled by the axemen of the then prince of Jodhpur.[28] One of the main reasons contributing to the emergence of Bishnoi beliefs was the overexploitation of the scanty resources of Rajasthan. The only way to safeguard the environment was to enunciate an ethic of conservation.

Founded by Guru Jambheshwar-ji Maharaj, Bishnoi religion has solely contributed to much of the greenery in arid Rajasthan. Wildlife has been able to sustain itself because of the attitudes the Bishnois have toward it. Bishnoi religion comprises twenty-nine principles (niyam) of which quite a few have direct relevance to the issues of environmental protection. For instance, their nineteenth principle prohibits the cutting of green trees; the twenty-third principle forbids Bishnois to castrate the bull, as it causes pain and injury to the animal; the twenty-eighth principle orders its followers to abstain from eating nonvegetarian food; the tenth principle submits that human beings should pardon others; the eleventh principle expects the Bishnois to be kind and compassionate to all around them, whether they are animals or plants; the twenty-second principle preaches that the Bishnois should take care of goats, sheep, and other benign animals.

Those who have conducted the studies of the Bishnois say that the principles that have a bearing on the environment are quite steadfastly followed, because of the growing consciousness among them that in case they do not save their environment, they are bound to suffer with a sharp decline in the essential things of life (such as water, food, and air). The educated and environmentally conscious Bishnois are spreading these ideas with further inputs from modern ecology. Bishnoi associations and interested individuals publish a number of periodicals in

---

28. See Ahmad (2002) and Srivastava (2003). Khushwant Singh (2002) suggests that arboricide (tree killing) should be treated in the same way as homicide is treated.

Hindi that regularly carry articles on the role of Bishnois in saving animal and plant life. The Bishnoi ethics of environmental protection and vegetarianism has exercised its impact on the other neighboring communities. It is also because the Bishnois are one of the economically powerful communities of Rajasthan and Haryana, and the castes that are dependent on them often change their lifestyles in the direction of their patrons.

There is an important difference between the Hindu and the Bishnoi attitude to nature. For Hindus, animals and plants are sensate beings—they have feelings and experience pain and pleasure—and therefore none of them should be harmed; this is the ideology of nonharming. But not all plants and animals are sacred, worthy of worship and veneration. The sacredness that is attributed to Pipal, or locally to banyan, is not attributed to other trees. Similarly, the sacredness of the cow is not extended to the camel despite its great use in deserts. Sacredness imposed on certain objects is independent of their material and commercial value. However, it should not be inferred from this that those animals and plants that are not sacred are worthy of condemnation. Whether they are the objects of ritual value or not, they all are to be protected.

In the Bishnoi system, by contrast, all natural entities are sacred, whether the tree is of Khejri or of a prickly type (such as Babul), or the animal is a cow or a deer. They all should be protected, even if it means giving up one's life, for they are sacred. The other communities in Rajasthan, and also the other parts of India, have the notion of a sacred piece of land (*oran*) and the trees that grow on it are not cut. In cases of violation, the punitive sanctions are assumed to come from deities and not human beings. In comparison to this, the Bishnois do not have the idea of a separate sacred grove. For them, the entire world is sacred. The human life acquires a transcendental meaning if it is sacrificed for the tasks of environmental protection. The popular publications on Bishnois carry articles on the martyrs who died while saving wildlife from the attack of poachers or trees from the contractors.

To sum up, the central idea in the Indian concept of nature is that it is a living entity. Various natural things—animals, plants, rivers, oceans—enter into a long-term relation with human beings, as is clear from the story of Śrī Rāmcharitramānas; therefore, they should be respectfully approached. The notion of community should not just be confined to human beings; rather, it should include all animals and plants. The notion of *vasudhā kutumbakam*— "the entire earth is my family"—is fundamental to the Indian notion of nature. The sensitivity, love, affection, and concern that emerge in the family are extended to everything that belongs to nature. In an interview, Chandi Prasad Bhatt, one of the architects of the Chipko movement, recalled that as a boy, when he walked through the alpine pasture, he "had to take off his shoes, so as not to harm the flowers." There existed a ban, he remembered, on spitting in Amrit Ganga because it polluted the river.[29] The traditions of folk ecology generate and sustain respect for nature, which is seen not in commercial but ritualistic terms. Conservation has been a part of the living traditions of many communities. In the villages of Rajasthan, when people want to wash their hands, "they go to a nearby plant or tree, wash their hands there, so that the used water does not go waste" (Srivastava, 1990, p. 292). The idea of regeneration of the environment or recycling its resources is paramount in these communities.[30]

---

29. See Guha (2002).

30. In one of her papers, Mead (1974) talked about the symbolic relationship that tribal societies have with their environment. In these symbols, the people talk about recycling. For example, the American Indian, who, after having eaten a fish, "put the bones back in the creek and said, 'Little brother, go back and be born again so I can eat you again' was symbolically talking about recycling" (p. 34).

Many Indian environmentalists think that ecological crises
have surfaced mainly because of the way in which human beings, completely consumed by the spirit of overuse, have treated
nature and her resources. One of the solutions suggested to resolve these crises is to spread the message of the traditional ethic,
besides improvising alternative technologies consistent with the
ideology of eco-preservation and sustenance. What is needed is
a blending of the religious and spiritual ideas with the benefits
of modern technology.

## REFERENCES

Ahmad, Meera. (2002). Bishnoi religion and nature. In *Religion and Environment*, Vol. II, Kishna Ram Bishnoi and Narsi Ram Bishnoi
(eds.), pp. 45–71. Hisar: Guru Jambheshwar University.

Bahuguna, Sunderlal. (1986). Technology vs. ecology. *The Hindustan
Times Sunday Magazine*, February 9.

*Bhagavad-Gita As It Is*. (2001). Translated by A. C. Bhaktivadanta Swami
Prabhupada. Mumbai: The Bhaktivadanta Book Trust.

Carrithers, Michael, and Humphrey, Caroline, eds. (1991). *The Assembly
of Listeners, Jains in Society*. Cambridge: Cambridge University Press.

Dundas, Paul. (1992). *The Jains*. London and New York: Routledge.

Farrar, Janet, and Farrar, Stewart. (1987). *The Witches' Goddess, The Femininity Principle of Divinity*. London: Robert Hale.

Guha, Ramachandra. (2002). A Gandhian in Garhwal. *The Hindu*, June
2 and 9.

Jaini, Padmanabh S. (1991). *Gender and Salvation: Jaina Sectarian Debates on
the Spiritual Liberation of Women*. Berkeley: University of California
Press.

Laidlaw, James. (1995). *Riches and Renunciation: Religion, Economy, and Society Among the Jains.* Oxford: Clarendon Press.

Luhrmann, T. M. (1989). *Persuasions of the Witch's Craft, Ritual Magic and Witchcraft in Present-Day England.* Oxford: Basil Blackwell.

Mead, Margaret. (1974). Changing perspectives on modernization. In *Rethinking Modernization, Anthropological Perspectives.* J. J. Poggie, Jr., and R. N. Lynch (eds.), pp. 21–36. Westport CT and London: Greenwood Press.

Mehra, J. D. (1987). Tribal India: continuity and change. In *India, Specially Published for the Festival of India in the U.S.S.R.* New Delhi: Brijbasi Printers.

Nance, Kevin. (1989). Worshiping the earth, nature-loving pagans fight negative image. *Lexington Herald-Leader,* July 18.

Ortner, Sherry. (1974). Is female to male as nature is to culture? In *Woman, Culture and Society,* M. Rosaldo and L. Lamphere (eds.). Stanford, CA: Stanford University Press.

Powers, John. (1995). *An Introduction to Tibetan Buddhism.* Ithaca, NY: Snow Lion Publications.

Roy Chakraverty, Ipsita. (1996). Wicca unveiled. *The Hindustan Times,* February 17.

Sarma, Nirupama. (1990). Throwing the angels out of business. *Independent,* January 14.

Siddiqui, Saleem. (2002). Islam and environment. In *Religion and Environment,* Vol. II. Kishna Ram Bishnoi and Narsi Ram Bishnoi (eds.), pp. 72–86. Hisar: Guru Jambheshwar University.

Singh, Khushwant. (2002). Tree killers. *The Hindustan Times,* September 14.

Srivastava, Vinay Kumar. (1988). Modern witchcraft and occultism in Cambridge. *Cambridge Anthropology* 13(1):50–71.

———. (1989). Some aspects of modern witchcraft and occultism. *Guru Nanak Journal of Sociology* 11(1):51–80.

———. (1990). In search of harmony between life and environment. *Journal of Human Ecology* 1(3): 291–300.

————. (1997). *Religious Renunciation of a Pastoral People*. New Delhi: Oxford University Press.

————. (2000a). On environment and culture. In *Man–Environment Relationship. Human Ecology Special Issue* No. 9, M. K. Bhasin and Veena Bhasin (eds.), pp. 13–20. Delhi: Kamla-Raj Enterprises.

————. (2000b). Social anthropology of pastoral nomads, the Raika Jati and its dharmic order. In *Studies on Man, Issues and Challenges*, M. K. Bhasin (ed.), pp. 281–298. Delhi: Kamla-Raj Enterprises.

————. (2000c). The rains and the Jains. *The Indian Express*, July 15.

————. (2001). Some thoughts on the anthropology of mental health and illness with special reference to India. *Bulletin of the Department of Anthropology, University of Dibrugarh* 29:21–47.

————. (2003). Some responses of communities to social tensions in India. *Anthropos* 98:157–165.

*The Holy Qur'an*. (1996). Translated into English by Abdullah Yusuf Ali. Hyderabad: Eliasii Family Book Service.

Tulsidās, Goswāmī. (2002a). *Srī Hanumān Chālīsā*, translated into English by Bharat Bhushan Srivastava. New Delhi: Aravali Books International

————. (2002b). *Sundarkānd of Sri Rāmcharitramānas*, translated into English by Bharat Bhushan Srivastava. New Delhi: Aravali Books International.

Usman, K. K., ed. (2001). *This Is Islam*. Cochin: Forum for Faith and Fraternity.

## ABOUT THE AUTHORS

CHEN SHAO-MING is a Professor of Chinese Philosophy at Zhongshan University, Canton. Chen recently published *The Interpreted Tradition in China*.

NADER EL-BIZRI is an Affiliated Research Scholar at the Department of History and Philosophy of Science at the University of Cambridge and a Research Associate in Philosophy at the Institute of Ismaili Studies in London. Of his scholarly writings, he has recently published *The Phenomenological Quest Between Avicenna and Heidegger* (GP, Binghamton, NY, 2000).

LEO MARX is Senior Lecturer and William R. Kenan Professor of American Cultural History Emeritus in the Program in Science, Technology, and Society at MIT. He is the author of many books, including *The Machine in the Garden* (1967), and *The Pilot and the Passenger: Essays on Literature, Technology, and Society in America* (1988).

JEAN-BERNARD OUÉDRAOGO teaches sociology in Burkina Faso at Université de Ouagadougou and Université Laval. His most recent publications are *Violence et communautés en Afrique noire.* (L'Harmattan, Paris, 1997) and *Arts photographiques en Afrique. Technique et esthétique dans la photographie de studio au Burkina Faso* (L'Harmattan, Paris, 2003).

VINAY KUMAR SRIVASTAVA teaches social anthropology at the University of Delhi. He is the author of *Religious Renunciation of a Pastoral People* (Oxford, 1997) and has edited *Methodology and Fieldwork* (Oxford, 2004). He has carried out intensive fieldwork in western Rajasthan, and is presently working on a book on the economy of a seminomadic, pastoral community.

PIERRE ZAOUI teaches philosophy at Université Paris X–Nanterre, and directs a program at the Collège International de Philosophie (Paris). He is the author of *Hume* (Editions les belles Lettres, 2005).

# KEYWORDS
**NADIA TAZI,** *Series Editor*

Other Press, in conjunction with five publishers from around the world, has launched the *Keywords* series. This five volume set offers different points of view on the cardinal ideas of Truth, Identity, Gender, Experience, and Nature. The series is being published simultaneously in Africa, the Arab World, China, France, India, and the United States in the languages native to these territories.

Carefully chosen authors from each of these territories have been given free rein to share their distinctive visions of the concept at hand. The variety of the authors' backgrounds (anthropology, philosophy, sociology, history, political science, and literature) and their commitment to making *Keywords* relevant in the explosive "here and now" offer new parameters for envisioning the implications of the process of globalization.

"A ready reckoner for the informed person."
— *The Statesman*, New Delhi

"An ambitious and very welcome venture."
—Simon Critchley, New School University

"Intercultural readings and contacts are a wonderful idea, but often difficult to achieve. The *Keywords* project is an imaginative way of helping us to deal with that problem. To understand the meaning of some basic concepts in different cultural settings is an interesting, provocative, and informative way of getting directly to the heart of different cultures."
—Daniel Callahan, Director of International Programs,
The Hastings Center

PREVIOUSLY PUBLISHED:

**Truth** | ISBN 1-59051-106-9 | Paperback with flaps | $15.00

**Identity** | ISBN 1-59051-105-0 | Paperback with flaps | $15.00

**Gender** | ISBN 1-59051-107-7 | Paperback with flaps | $15.00

**Experience** | ISBN 1-59051-108-5 | Paperback with flaps | $15.00